Egg Time in Augusta

And wake to the farm forever fled from the childless land.
Oh as I was young and easy in the mercy of his means,
Time held me green and dying
Though I sang in my chains like the sea.

—Dylan Thomas, *Fern Hill*

Egg Time

In Augusta

Hugh Roth

Polar Bear & Company
An imprint of the
Solon Center for Research and Publishing
Solon & Rockland, Maine

Polar Bear & Company™
Solon Center for Research and Publishing
PO Box 311, Solon, ME 04979
20 Main Street, Rockland, ME 04841
207.643.2795, polarbearandco.org, soloncenter.org

Original cover art by Wanatha Garner, design by Ramona du Houx.
Photos courtesy author's collection.
ISBN: 978-1-882190-79-9
Library of Congress Control Number: 2017954868
First print edition, first printing December 2017
Manufactured on acid-free paper in more than one country.

For my children,

Rachel
Evan
David

Contents

Author's Note

Church Hill Road

My editor thought it appropriate as well as useful that I provide an explanation of the frequent changes that signal an abrupt narrative shift: a discussion with an invisible acquaintance, a change in perspective, an internal monologue, a theatrical aside.

Their literary identity is easier to explain than their literary necessity. Comments from the grownup that I am, about the actual events or the actual meaning of those events, are in *italics*. The text of a discussion is further set off from the main text of the narrative with Gill Sans Light.

The necessity for the author to go careening through his own story, a story which is often playing simultaneously on different levels, is, simply, that in no other way could I tell it. The reasons are the very fabric of the story, as I think you will find; further explanations are just diversions.

Some chapters of the story shift to the third person. A friend suggested that "first person" sacrificed too much, particularly in that it burdened the narrator with telling the reader everything, and that such a multi-threaded story could be handled both more richly and more naturally in the third person. But I found, after some considerable work, that parts just didn't work well without the immediacy of the first person. And so the mix.

I must explain here, loudly, that this is a work of fiction. If you think you see yourself referenced in proximity to some of the events retold here, you don't. You see my imagination at work. It is simply that an author must start *somewhere*.

The book started with a three-page sketch about the incubators in the kitchen, written longhand in the library of Queens College while my son Evan took some sort of entrance exam. Scattered among the twenty years I have taken to finish the book, years of great personal growth and change, are the three I actually spent writing it. These years were also a time of learning about my parents, their beginnings, their artistic endeavors, and their stories of the life, now so many years ago, that we led on Church Hill Road and elsewhere in Maine. The book is richer for that knowledge.

I want to say first that the book simply would not have been possible to write without the years of help from Diane Eaton of Woodmere, NY.

Although my parents are no longer here, some old friends survive who shared their stories, among them Tom Foster, Dan Field, Alton Fuller, Olive Edwards, and Pam Braley. In addition, I would like to thank John Wiley, Charlene Donahue of the Maine State Entomology Lab, John Drury of Vinalhaven, the Kennebec Historical Society, the staff of the Maine State Library, and Cindy Kuhn of the Fields Pond Audubon Center for their consideration and help.

I would like to thank the authors of some of the resources of which I took advantage. Among them are:

Marilyn J. Dwelley: books on flowers
Stan Tekiela: *Birds of Maine*
Richard Dickinson and France Royer: *Weeds of North America*
Peterson First Guide: *Wildflowers*
Else and Hans Hvass: *Mushrooms and Toadstools*
Alexander Martin: *Weeds*
David Allen Sibley: *The Sibley Guide to Birds*
Glen H. Mittelhauser et al.: *The Plants of Acadia National Park*
The Peterson audio guide to bird calls and sounds

Vinalhaven, Maine   H.R.
March, 2017

The Clock

Kitchen interior, Augusta.

I think it was the clock, the electric clock that sat all those years in the kitchen on that little painted shelf, the clock with the squat, mean-looking face (too small to tell you the time at a glance), and with its cord threaded down through a hole, the extra gathered underneath in a neat bow, the clock with its dusty, plastic case, in some faded, nondescript pastel, its faint grinding noise when everything else was still, and its array of knurled knobs standing out from the back which demanded touching and turning and which reached down into the clock's dark innards, the clock that ticked off the minutes and the hours and the days and the years and watched a succession of difficult and embarrassing and improbable events, and never said anything. And because it hunkered down and pretended to be busy, to concentrate on what it was doing while maintaining the faint smile of myopia and friendship, and to look out the window a lot—at what I can't imagine; at the tops of some alders off in the distance?—because of these reasons, it has been left to me to tell the story.

I have also tried for years to avoid telling it—amused myself in a number of interesting ways, learned whole careers and then tossed them aside, disappeared off one side of the screen like some tiresome video game character and reappeared on the other, anticipating new horizons. They were always the same. I never knew how to locate those embedded symbols of magical power. I occasionally resorted to desperate and unpopular reimagings, only to discover, finally, that which I always knew without knowing: I am that story, and that through all these new paths and giddy transformations, I have been merely sitting on a shelf displaying the time with the alarm set forever at 5:15.

Oh, I had some knowledge of the clock. At each juncture in this road of years, I opened the clock and patiently took apart the—no, the details are not important—I'm sure you know all you want to about armatures and escape wheels and torus-shaped coils of copper wire bound in a crisscrossed fashion like the Roman fasces. The triumphant reassembling of the clock—it always started (I'm a fairly careful worker)—held great promise. The more effort, however, I put into realizing that promise, the more difficult it became to continue, until finally, like the years when I used to walk by the clock and try to read the time, I abandoned the effort.

Several years ago the clock stopped. I hadn't looked at it in several weeks—who understands these things? Just tired, I suppose, or worn out waiting for someone to listen. And no, I hadn't had it apart in a long time! When did it stop? you might ask, seeking to ascribe some special significance to the time. No. Unlike for Miss Havisham, the time is of no particular significance—and I couldn't give you an answer anyway, because when I bothered to look at it at all, the time was always different. Never knowing what time it is creates a lack of clarity—events and feelings and perspectives and roles percolate up through the karst of everyday life. The sinkholes of the world are large. I am my parents and my children: like the four-faced creatures on the corners of Ezekiel's chariot, I look in all directions.

The great failing of these creatures is that they never look down, so for them our suffering and loss remains invisible or an abstraction. Unless you look down, you will never gain empathy. They will learn it one day, but, like Lear, they will pay a terrible price. As Brünnhilde says in her final indictment: "Look down, oh you mighty gods, and behold your eternal guilt!"

That is why I talk to myself so much, why I ask so many questions: there is so much explaining to do. For this I must ask your indulgence. I see back to the beginning, back through all those years as if through a very long tunnel, at first as apparently empty as a silo in June. Yet look! Stacked like poker chips of hazy air are those years, each one different, yet that difference is as difficult to explain as the differences in the layers of a cake when they are all vanilla. Such clarity is useful, even remarkable, but such clarity comes at a price: the stages of my life do not exhibit the usual boundaries, the demarcations of surprise and wonder, nor the milestones crossed and left behind, milestones sonorously reviewed at public demonstrations of faith and continuity and informed with great meaning toward which all the listeners strain, but whose significance eludes them. Later, in more private conversations, the listeners will fall back on the steadier ground of abstraction—or maybe the concrete—it's so much easier to talk about a new outboard motor than the meaning of life, to stay in close at some level of detail rather than "out there," where generalizations form and edgy skepticism lies in wait. The most comfortable comments are the ones with their own inherent contradictions, or those resting unsteadily on landfills of decomposing assumptions: "I wish I could get Johnny to read more."

One can only murmur in sympathetic agreement.

But, enough of milestones. Again, I ask your indulgence. I am like an emotionally-driven maggot, debriding the suppurating edges of a loosening scab, the patient construction of which has been the work of a lifetime, and whose attachment, at this point, can only be maintained by busying myself with what the world expects. By the time you finish reading this, it will have fallen off. I want it never to heal. The questions I ask myself are an encouragement, a kind of agreement that the work is worthwhile, or to help me remember what I don't want to remember, or to give over something that is mine in some unshareable way. I also ask you to keep in mind that the penalty for telling you this story is death.

Introduction

Up north, the winters are long: spring comes haltingly, its forward progress often invisible, its slush interminable, and it backslides into winter with a total lack of concern. Having promised nothing, it delivers less. But, as the noonday sun moves higher in the sky, the frozen earth slowly relents, and the blanketing snow thins. Spots of grass appear, holes of matted vegetation. The spots march across a field like the holes in a cooking pancake, spreading, growing, until amoeba-like, they join others. For a day, for a week, irregularly shaped patches of snow between the growing bare areas persist, like the dough left behind by a cookie cutter. Why is the dough that is left so much more important than the cookies? Intersecting arcs create crosses of asymptotes, islands of dough; sharply pointed peninsulas occasionally connect over springy tombolos. The dough aches for what is not.

Knot-like holes, eroded from underneath, appear in the icy plates that grip the driveway. Meltwater, a slow if brutally cold carborundum, shapes the receding edges into soft curves that belie their knife-life sharpness, much like the fluting in the Vishnu Schist along the Colorado. The high banks of snow at the side of the road shrink grudgingly. Each night they freeze, and in their frozen hearts conspire to live forever. The sun's light is mechanical and devoid of graciousness—its indifferent warmth the melting snow absorbs as dry sand does an ocean wave. Icy runoff fills the ditches; arroyos, formed years ago in the long-suffering gravel shoulders of the road, flood. Here a large one slopes quickly to the ditch, carrying everything but the larger stones; there, slower water creates a miniature delta. A delicate sandbar glistens in the sun. Mud is everywhere.

After the snow, the land lies exhausted. Everything is wet, cold and wet, the fields soggy, the ditches flowing, the lakes brimming, the brook wide and surging, drowning the swale at its edges. From a gently swaying cattail comes the brassy trill and the purest whistle: the redwing blackbirds are back! In town, the end of the guardrail at the west end of the Water Street parking lot lies, yet again, submerged by the rising Kennebec River. And so it remains to this day; they never have figured out how to fix it.

Nor have I. That pitted, rusty guardrail near the river rips into my flesh, like guardrails everywhere, with the ugly debris and scrub weeds and cigarette butts under them protected by their raw, utilitarian construction whose edges I use to hack up my body. And, oh God! the guardrail where Pam Bradley and I sat waiting for the Cony High marching band to form up, she with her hand in mine, or maybe her elbow on my shoulder, and oh my God! you could see the edge of her bra through her sleeveless blouse, and, oh! to be loved, to get that reflected look, that unfulfilled desire, now seen as one might from the back of the last car of a train as it moves away, slowly. Let me be a guardrail like that one, with no beginning, with my back to the Bangor Street bridge, with my back to the mysterious river, like that one, sloping up out of the rising water. Let me hide in one of its hollow posts, among the spider webs and the sharp-threaded, angry, aluminum bolts, or maybe in the end, the end spiraled like a Corinthian volute, where I could grow, nautilus-like and secure, sharing its coiled potential. Warmed by the sun on bright spring days, I can comment at length about the comings and goings of that parking lot, about families walking up to Water Street to buy a graduation suit at Farrell's, about those who fail to park within the yellow lines, about the activity at the Sears loading dock, and about those who stare at the river from the high office windows. Let me hide there—of course, I would never look up when a girl happened to step across to sit with her boyfriend—like Pam and I did— (how could you think it?) hide there so as not to have to mention the visits on winter evenings in that poorly-lit loading dock, Clearance 11'6", *hidden among massive concrete pillars, and the four of us in that ugly Chevrolet Suburban, waiting to load something nobody really wanted, when I think (endlessly revisited)* and Mommy doesn't want this, *and, oh! let me drag my mouth across that vile, pitted guardrail, let me die before I utter the least sound, the smallest complaint, before I have to bring in the bedding, cold and still slightly damp and heavy with the smell of urine, from the clothesline and make my bed. We drive out of the parking lot and across the low bridge and up the hill and past Williams School with its high windows, reflective and uninviting, and I hate that place, and* they watch me from those windows—I *smash them* (such poor decorum) *and I slash my fingers* (please don't make a mess) *with their hot, jagged edges. And so, bleeding, out of town, driving along with whatever it was that we picked up that nobody wants, in a van that nobody likes, to a house in which nobody wants to live, to use whatever we bought to fix what nobody wants to own. The streetlights thin, then give out entirely, and we are in a darkened van on a country road. Occasional headlights pass us by.*

The car stops. The house is dark and inert; we struggle out. The healing begins—scabs form quickly in the country. Tomorrow will be better. Mommy starts supper. Chores.

Part I

The Places

All these places are no more: burnt down, bulldozed, gone. But in a past endlessly reclaimed only to be lost again, they are remembered as they once were.

Ya todos los caminos están cerca,
Y hasta el camino del milagro
(Now all roads are near,
Even the road of dreams.)

—Jorge Luis Borges,
Calle con almacén rosado

Chapter I

The House in Center Montville

A rambling, nineteenth-century farmhouse one-and-a-half miles from Route 3: white, green trim, two big trees out front, a big barn in some state of disrepair, and 105 acres. About $1,200 in 1946. Water, in warm weather, came from a spring and flowed via a wooden trough into a barrel down by the shed. A barrel and a party-line phone and a kitchen stove sum up the utilities when we moved in, but the road was on the to-do list of the Rural Electrification Administration, and electricity at some point arrived. How far it actually got into the house must remain a mystery. No-name dirt road—now a bit pretentiously renamed North Ridge Road.

Daddy drove us up Memorial Day weekend and drove back to Boston to continue in the newspaper delivery job he had managed to find, after either quitting or possibly being laid off from his wartime machinist job. He spoke years later that he might have held on to it if he had been able to tolerate the bourgeois implications of that holding on, but the reality remains unclear.

He came back in September, having received a desperate call from my mother that he must come home.

"So he had left you alone? How old were you?"

"Not yet three, Jeb not yet five."

"So he left you and your brother and your mother alone in a strange house on a road where you knew no one, no car, no running water, no electricity, no grocery store? Is that how it was?"

"Yeah, you got it. But keep in mind that this was Paradise."

Years later, in Albuquerque, their mobile home, their first new home and the first with running hot water, was in a park called Paradise Acres. How fitting—

————

"What'd you go to Maine for, anyway?"

"Daddy had spent a summer writing *Call It Sleep* in Norridgewock, a small town north and west of where we were, so he knew of Maine. And we had to get out of Somerville—or wherever the firetrap we were living in was—because the doctor suggested that a change of environment might cure Jeb's stutter."

We lived that winter on his $25 unemployment check and money earned by helping the farmer next door in the woods. The following spring, my father decided to dig a ditch from the wellspring to the shed. The rocks in Maine soil are bad enough, but at about fifteen inches you hit hardpan, a layer of compressed clay that is impervious to a shovel (and impervious to water as well). You have to use a pickax, and by received wisdom you have to go down five feet to be absolutely sure that even on the bitterest winter day, the pipe will not freeze. When this proved too arduous, Gene Perry, the farmer next door with whom Daddy had worked in the winter, suggested dynamite and offered to help him with the blasting. He got a signed form from one of the town selectmen, and took it to the local hardware store; out he came with dynamite, blasting caps, and some fuse. He put us in the barn, in case a stray rock went through one of the house windows. I remember watching through a crack and seeing the two of them bend down to light the fuse, and then, here they come, at a dead run. After the explosion, a few rocks landed on the barn roof. Several decades later when I was working on a survey crew for the Maine State Highway Commission, we had to measure the water level of any working well near a blasting site, because the impact of the explosion radiating down into the ground could close up the underground channels on which the well's usefulness depended.

"Survey crew. That must have been interesting."

"Interesting but painful. It was the first time that I had to learn something new in an unfamiliar environment, something new that was physical *and* intellectual. It also marked the first appearance of a disability—I don't think that's too strong a word—that has followed me my whole life. Actually, in a real sense, it followed me for more than my whole life, because this inability to act, this making poor judgment calls, this throwing the self up in the way of making a reasoned decision, this analysis and reanalysis of everything, was an affliction of my father's for which he never failed to savage himself."

"So you just kind of hooked onto it, so to speak?"

"Yes. Erik Erikson says someplace, maybe in *Youth: Crisis and Identity*, that the superego is not so much built up from experience as transferred intact—fully formed, as it were—from the parent."

"How did this disability show up in you?"

"Unlike for others, a skill and its necessary knowledge were never incorporated in the self, and without such incorporation, this skill and knowledge failed to provide a sense of competence, of mastery, and so failed to fuel the confidence to act. The psychic kentledge that I trundled around left little space for learning or acting: its maintenance drained away every ounce of available energy. Actions and decisions were invariably mediated: such mediation produced a hesitation, and, as I was always watching myself, the hesitation was inevitably interpreted as a lack of confidence, and so the process grew on itself, as very small movements of air can develop into of a cyclone. I could never be spontaneous when others were around. I enjoyed doing things by myself because then all I had to account for was some extra time, and I could experiment, I could do things repeatedly until I could explain them well and do them well and do them efficiently, but the efficiency was not to get the job done quickly, but rather so that I could do the job without analysis. The more I tried to act, the heavier this psychic weight became. I already spoke about this in the very beginning, in the metaphor about the clock."

"Oh, that's like your father's explanation of the physics of trying to make something go faster than the speed of light."

"Yeah, it's a painfully apt metaphor: As an object approaches the speed of light, a greater and greater proportion of the energy driving it is converted to mass. So as the object approaches the speed of light, the mass of the object approaches infinity. How could I function all these years with such a weight? I can only say that I would not suffer such torture again."

"But you did learn a lot, no?"

"Yes, I was way smarter than many of the people with whom I worked: I remembered stuff, I absorbed details, I was intellectually acquisitive, I made connections. But instead of becoming an integrated asset which I could parley, say, into a better position, the knowledge was cordoned off. It was never mine. I never shone. I was like a singer who never used the bottom half of his lungs. This is how, as I said earlier, I learned whole careers and then tossed them aside. They were external. I have explained this psychic drama to others by comparing it to an eight-cylinder engine. On a normal day, I hit on four cylinders."

"And what were the other cylinders doing?"

"Deadweight—just siphoning off power—they powered the business of existing, instead of the business of living."

"And what did you have to do to use more?"

"They were not available—took years of working with Diane to be able to use them at all. But I learned other new stuff on the survey crew, because it was the first time I worked with other men and could listen to what they talked about, what they were interested in."

"And what did you find?"

"The main topics of discussion were alcohol, pussy, work, automobiles, the last job, the next job, food, and stories of (most likely apocryphal) illegal activities of mythic proportions that were never found out. I was embarrassed by their talk, kidded about not focusing enough on the useful parts of a woman's anatomy, and ridden for being a Jew."

"How bad was the Jew-baiting?"

"Not bad, really. There was a guy on the crew named Hy or maybe Henry Kendall who most often brought up the subject. Other than the normal prejudices of working-class Gardiner, he had been a car salesman, and I'm sure he was constantly having his deals taken out from under him by Jews or by dealerships owned by Jews. If he had been successful he would not have felt the need to be so dismissive of others on the crew or have come to work at all for the State Highway Commission at $52.50 a week, which was the starting salary, and, married, being forced to live in a motel for the week when too far from home, and since Maine is a big state, that was often."

"Who else was on the crew?"

"The crew chief's name was Danny Sweet. I think he was an engineering student at UMaine who was taking some time off—maybe because his wife had a baby. Smart enough guy—pleasant. I could have learned a lot from him. But, you see, that's the point: I could know a great deal but never be a crew chief, because to be a crew chief you had to act based on what was in front of your face, not on some ideal, be it ever so beautifully constructed. The fourth was Larry Poulin, who had graduated from a tech school and who was a member of the Air National Guard. I thought that was kind of cool. First time I heard a French Canadian savage his own people—'just a dumb Frenchman,' he would say of someone. I couldn't imagine saying something so offensive. Funny—in no other job do I remember the people so clearly."

"Did you feel that some of the people you worked with were your friends?"

"I don't know about friends ... maybe more recently. For most of my life I have been such a fake ... people must have sensed something was wrong and kept their distance. I certainly wouldn't be a friend to the person that I was."

The second winter we had running water as far as the shed. I put my mouth on the naked, metal pipe to get a drink, and my lips froze to it. I had to be torn away from it. The next summer, Daddy piped water into the kitchen sink.

Above the spring, the land steepened, part of it exposed rock from whose cracks grew blue, bell-shaped, flowers—

actually called bluebells.

I remember them because my mother said they were kind of rare, and we shouldn't pick them. It was at the top of this hill, as it rounded away from the steeper area, where we would sit on the warm rock amid junipers and lichens and pick wintergreen-flavored teaberry leaves to chew on. Further back, at the very top of the hill, was a maple grove. We tapped the trees and collected the sap. There was a brick-lined fire pit with a big, shallow pan for the initial cooking down of the sap. The sap, so reduced, would then be finished on the kitchen stove. My mother managed to spill boiling maple syrup on one of her hands—just punishment, I suppose, for failing to practice piano regularly. She wore cotton gloves on Vaselined hands to bed for years after. We had some goats. My father built an electrified fence, and he allowed me to touch it. Like the maple syrup, just another punishment.

The second winter he taught at the local one-room school, another job which he hated. An older girl, teasing, pulled off Jeb's hat and threw it on the ground. Daddy slapped her. That night, her brothers came around the house to scare us. Daddy went out with the shotgun. They took off. He fired over their heads. They didn't come back. We fit right in.

Chapter II

The House in West Washington, 1948–9

The house was the Maine equivalent of a sharecropper's shack: raw, weathered boards, no electricity, and water that had to be hand drawn from a well and brought into the kitchen, where on cold nights it froze. No phone if there was an emergency. My mother, alone, with two small children.

At the hands of what angry God were we left to live in a place like that? She reported that growing up, she was allowed neither to cry nor to complain.

No car—the car being used by my father to commute to his job at the Augusta State Hospital. He stayed there during his weeklong shift, then came home on his day off.

I should point out, not too sourly I hope, that at the hospital he had a warm dormitory room and a hot shower.

Grocery store a mile away, down on Route 17. We ended up there because it was the only place to rent within walking distance of the one-room schoolhouse in which she taught that year. We had some goats. In the winter we all slept in one bed to stay warm. We had been warned not to use the fireplace—the chimney was not to be trusted. The next tenants failed to listen, and the place burned down. Jeb was seven, and so he went to school. I went to school, too, but in good weather my mother would give me a nickel after lunch and allow me to walk down to the store—the trip kept me occupied. So it was a two-mile walk for some candy—alone, five years old, on a little-used road. I suppose in the winter I stayed by the stove at school. Several times I remember running into a flock of chickens that had wandered onto the road, and I was so scared of them (and particularly the rooster) that I would not walk by. In pictures, my brother and I make the Joad kids look spiffy.

How was it we did not die there—there in the old house in West Washington? I have always yearned for death because I could not fix what my parents lacked.

Seems there was some sort of manmade pond in the back. Beyond, some way up a modest hill, my brother started building a log cabin, and despite his age, used a saw, and possibly even a hatchet. I remember we went up there once or twice with Daddy so he could help Jeb with some of the construction. There was an abandoned sawmill nearby—who knows how dangerous the place was—where we played and dug in the sawdust piles. Paradise? Yes, but the price was very high. My father later allowed as how living like this built character.

Chapter III

Augusta

O ur house lay most of the way down a steep hill. Once past it, the road bottomed smoothly over a brook, the lowest place on the road, before regaining some of its height with an easy climb up past the church, then roughly north, wandering quickly out of sight on its way to no place in particular: the back way to Vassalboro, I guess, or in the summer, Webber Pond. You have seen similar houses: white clapboards, green shutters, the add-on phases of its construction obvious, a barn set back a hundred feet or so, various outbuildings, the function of most of them obvious. A few unkempt acres surrounded the house, all of them sloping to some degree toward the brook, which in the spring was a torrent, expansive and self-important, but in August a turbid trickle, minding its own business, trying to stay cheerful like the head of the Chamber of Commerce of a once-prosperous small town now fallen on hard times.

In summer, the exposed banks of the brook lie open—silt-brown flesh baked clay-hard in the hot sun—lie open to the gaze of casual passersby. After a rain they glisten as if coated with mucous. Such nakedness—I look away.

Church Hill Road was one of dozens just like it all over the state—just a way to get from here to there, the there's never too well known even to the residents, else they would have taken a different route. No street sign, no route number, no particular landmarks. In those years it still balanced uneasily between a place to live and a place to work. Every morning Fred Cunningham drove his herd of milk cows down the road to pasture and yup, drove them home at night, their stretched-out udders swinging back and forth, pendulously answering every lurching step—a sad bunch of bandy-legged ruminants. Some years before the town had upgraded the existing dirt road, smoothed out the profile some, straightened a few bad curves, put in culverts to carry water across the road, and cut ditches on each side to improve drainage. Then they paved it. Every winter the road self-destructed, partly from the frost and partly from the pounding of the snowplows and the overweight logging trucks on their way to Hudson Pulp and Paper. In the spring, hunks of pavement lay scattered on our lawn. Every summer road crews came around and patched it, but were often reduced to patching the patches.

The town, at the request of the fire department, had put in a dam just where our brook went under the road: the ponded water could resupply a pumper in case of a fire, as the nearest hydrant was four miles away. A big culvert carried the crashing spillway water under the road, where it then wandered slowly through pines, toadstools, and fallen trees. The far shore of the brook, overhung with alders, sloped rather sharply up, then across a field to Gilley's place, an imposing building whose combination of black, oversized trim, high walls, and off-white, asbestos siding gave it a feeling of exposure.

One should never see a house's foundations, the narrow, clerestory windows peering into darkness and the raw, unfinished, concrete—even the Bible says it: "and he shall see her nakedness and she shall see his nakedness, it is a disgrace; he shall bear his iniquity." I hope I don't have to say anything more—you get the idea.

A single tree stood off to one side of Gilley's place: no architectural details relieved its stark squareness, softened neither by landscaping nor balanced by outbuildings. One got a feeling of hollowness, of nothing behind the oversized, curtainless windows, a feeling only increased by the fact that it was empty during most of the years we lived on the road. People came by once in a while, then disappeared. An older man we met there once breathed wheezingly, his speech rasping and compressed as if trying to speak while holding his breath. Ernest told us that the second floor was so open and spacious they used to have dances there, and, his face lightening a bit, "a hell'uva good time."

"Ever go over there?"
"After the fire, we went over there only one other time."
"The fire? What fire?"
"The grass fire that got away from Daddy."
"How'd it start? This isn't the one you told me about, is it?—when you and Allen were smoking near the barn and—"
"No, no, that was different. Daddy deliberately started the fire—"
"Started a fire? Started a fire in the grass near your neighbor's house?

What'd he start a fire for?"

"To burn off last year's matted grass so new grass would grow better, so the ducks and geese could forage more, so we wouldn't have to buy so much grain to fatten them up."

Ernest Cunningham was our immediate up-the-hill neighbor. A product of the rural Maine of the nineteenth century, and already a young man by 1900, he owned hundreds of acres of fields and woodlands stretching away to the east behind our houses. His house, beginning with the parlor on the end closest to the road and ending with the manure pile at the other, had that cobbled-together air of necessity and poverty.

Across the road—to the west of us—was a wreck of a house sitting in a large field, at the end of which was the family cemetery, long abandoned, of the eponymous Churches. Before zooming by you might have noticed a dirt road off to the left, next to that field, also going west. A single, unmaintained lane of gravel and exposed rock, Blair Road was a badly rutted remnant of a once-busier countryside. The wrecked house collapsing into its cellar was emblematic of this contraction—the roof tipped back, and the single, second-floor window looked blankly up at the morning sun. Next to the house was a dense thicket of lilacs. You could still make out the lines of the old driveway, now softened and completely grassed over. Days went by without a passing car, and the occasional one you did see was usually that of a couple, the young man intent on finding an undisturbed place to demonstrate his limitless affection. This demonstration usually lasted as long as the beer. In the morning, the ambit of their passion could be judged by the area of matted-down grass: if it was about the size of a coffin, the under-mentionables had come off without significant trouble, and the beer bottles were close by; if it was the size you would expect from say, a large moose, the beer bottles were scattered around in the tall grass, the arc of love having given them wings.

Our house stretched back from the road, the oldest pieces built in the nineteenth century, the newer pieces cobbled on in a rather disjointed fashion, the whole of it with the years achieving a certain softness of line: slight buckles, gentle sags, corners not quite square. Little had been done to improve it—upgrading was a concept then inching its way north from Connecticut. Most noticeable from the road was a wide, L-shaped porch, wrapped around the southwest corner, whose sloping roof was supported by handsome wooden columns standing on a wide railing. In the spring we put up large, wood-framed screens which sat on this same railing: they were ungainly, oblong affairs, whose mitered joints had been limbered by years of use. The largest of them had a door; all were held in place by strategically placed latch hooks. To sit on this now-bug-free porch was a real pleasure, the summer evening softly exhaling, fading, the old elm near the ruined house outlined against the setting sun. After . dark nut-hard June bugs crashed into the screen. Fat-bodied moths with dusty, mud-brown wings flew around and around the light-bulbs until they dropped from exhaustion. Soon after dark, it was time for a sweater; by ten o'clock the chill night air drove you inside. Once a robin built a nest in the eaves of the porch before we put up the screens. The poor mother became frantic when she could no longer get to the nest. We took it down, a little basket of pleached sticks and mud and a few feathers; it held four tiny eggs with leathery shells, eggs of such a unique blue that the world needs no other definition. Put the color into words, and you no longer have it. At the near corner of the porch was a bushy lilac, which on June nights breathed forth its intoxicating smell. This bush, like all the other trees and plants and attempts at beautifying the property remained, except for their natural growth, untended and unimproved.

Parallel to the driveway and at the foot of the garden was a large bed of narcissus, a perennial with a pretty, white flower. A forest of them appeared every May, and this without attention or fertilizer. If we were lucky, they were at their most prolific just before Memorial Day. Jeb, ever the more frugal and cagey son, put out a sign and started selling them. But business did not boom until Daddy ran an ad in the local paper, with the result that the flowers were all sold by one p.m. on the day after the ad. In a good year we sold maybe 120 dozen at 35 cents each. No colorful floral wrap for us—we used wax paper. People were glad to get inexpensive flowers for "Decoration Day"—inexpensive and fresh. We usually cut them while customers waited. Closer to the road was a row of peonies, in the other direction a hydrangea. On the far side of the narcissus, on a gentle slope up toward Ernest's, was our garden. The plot had nothing to recommend it save that it wasn't used for anything else: it was too tightly bordered for farm machinery to be truly effective, yet it was too large to prepare by hand.

We moved to Augusta in late August, 1949. My father, a writer not writing and just marking time, worked as an attendant at the Augusta State Hospital. My mother, a pianist without a piano, had gotten a job teaching in the one-room schoolhouse in Chelsea, a neighboring town. Our Model A Ford—

Model A's were last manufactured in 1932—

was, until we demolished it, parked in a rickety, unpainted shed standing between the house and the barn; running water was a pump in the kitchen; a big chicken coop sat out by the road; the back of the house had several small structures of unknown function stuck to it like parasites. Despite its shortcomings, it was a big improvement from our two previous houses in Maine, especially from the more pathetic one in West Washington.

There was more, I'm sure, but I was little—at six, only some stuff sticks. My brother has found a cleaner, possibly even better way of handling those years. He remembers nothing.

Daddy was five foot eight inches with a big chest, wire-rimmed glasses, bad teeth, psoriasis, and bursitis. He cut into his leg with a hatchet working in the woods the first winter in Maine, and it never fully healed. The injury is not surprising: the snow between your gloves and the handle act like icy ball bearings, and worse, he was using it left-handed. Gene Perry, our neighbor and, I learned years later, a friend, had bought a two-man, war-surplus chainsaw. Daddy worked with him cutting wood—felling trees without a stitch of safety equipment. I cringe at the thought of him floundering in hip-deep snow, holding the south end of that monster. What with the resistance of the snow and the hidden limbs and vines waiting to catch your boots, and the high-cut stumps of small trees with their frost-hardened edges that will gouge your flesh, with these lurking beneath the surface, simply attempting to move is among the most demoralizing activities you can imagine. I have worked in the winter woods in

Henry, Kitchen, Augusta, 1955

Maine; we, at least, had snowshoes and a truck with a heater. I remember he had one tie, wool challis, green. I look for wool challis ties in stores: they never have them.

Mommy was five foot ten inches, square shoulders, big hands, 145 pounds, no curves, straight, brown hair worn simply, a painful hip since her late twenties, an ulcer that wouldn't heal, bad varicose veins, poor circulation in her legs. She bought men's tie shoes from Sears for her wide feet. Her striking, youthful elegance had faded.

My brother Jeremy was almost eight, thin, a couple of inches taller than me, goofy looking, ears sticking out a bit, distant; disdainful. He held his body with a hunched stiffness—you can still see this in photos twenty-five years later. He entered the third grade at Williams School on Bangor Street in Augusta. We called him Jeb.

I was six and considered chubby, mostly because of my big face. Overly sensitive, somewhat more social, and silly, the silliness covering a multitude of other problems—and happy to fail at just about everything.

And if I could not fail at it, I lost interest and tossed it down.

I entered the first grade at this same school. Both of us had amblyopia, Jeremy particularly, a condition guaranteed to make you look a bit odd and to sink any hopes you might have of playing sports, since you have no depth perception.

Winter shrank our already small house by making the unheated rooms useful only for storage. The two bedrooms upstairs remained as we found them, their spareness unrelieved by decoration, and their utility signaling that rest and sleep were merely something to get done with so you could move on with the business of life. The floor was of boards, slightly cupped, and these edges telegraphed their presence through the linoleum, which was eventually softened with some sisal runners. There was one light—at the top of the stairs: my parents found their way using a flashlight. Otherwise not a picture, not a curtain. For the entire floor: two closets and a clothes rack. On cold mornings, a heavy frost coated the inside of our window, and this despite the wood-framed storm windows, whose installation and removal were part of the ritual of every fall and spring. We kept the door at the top of the stairs closed in the winter to keep the heat downstairs. Early in the morning, the kitchen was the only warm room, the furnace having died down during the night. Everyone dressed there. I took a deep breath, bolted out of bed, grabbed my clothes, and flew down the stairs. The house was really warm only once in the winter: the February it burnt down.

The living room—so we called it—had two armchairs and one settee, all made out of bent cedar. It was actually patio furniture, but we never mentioned that fact, so no one knew. My mother made pads out of blue corduroy for the bottoms and the backs, so the chairs' ribs didn't poke you. The settee had a couple of throw pillows and was for company, thin company. Two fourteen-year-old boys fit nicely. Today that furniture sits on a porch in Bangor, Maine; it looks to be the proper size for a tree house. Book shelves, L-shaped, occupied one corner. On the wall was a copy of the famous picture of Brahms at the piano with his cigar-stained beard, only it was just part of the original: the rest had been cut off to fit the frame. We eventually got a hi-fi, so the settee had to be moved. The hi-fi was made for those decorators who wanted to keep its real use a secret: eighty percent furniture, twenty percent electronics. Here also were the stairs up to the bedrooms.

The last heated room, off the living room, was the "den," primarily a place for my father to work at his desk. On the weekends it was a place to set up a card table for a game or a tea party. Along one wall we hung the artwork we brought home from school. Various cases, shelves and chests of drawers stood against the wall, contents mysterious or off limits. In the corner was a built-in breakfront. Fancy dishes above, tablecloths and such below. You knew we were pulling out all the entertainment stops when my mother went there to get things. Also in this room was the door to the cellar, a dank, dark space with stone walls, a gravel floor, and a low, sometimes painfully low, ceiling.

During the winter we lived in these three rooms. They originally surrounded a large pantry, which we soon converted into a bathroom.

On the other side of the living room, facing the road, was the front parlor. We called it the library; in it was a desk and my mother's music cabinet and, eventually, her piano. Books, I think, on the far wall. In the other direction, behind the kitchen, was an L-shaped hallway at the end of which was the privy. And finally, beyond the ell and the back door, was an enclosed space that had no floor and which was originally used to store coal or firewood. It was a scary place, so dark that it was easy to imagine stepping over the threshold of its entrance door and, finding no floor, flopping face down into the raw dirt, four feet below. The house was a symphony of forced utility, low ceilings, and linoleum. Years later my parents let some relatives use the house for the summer. They took the seats out of their Volkswagen bus so they would have something comfortable to sit on. Upholstery had arrived, but a bit too late. At the end of August, it drove away.

Upstairs, my brother and I slept on army cots. One of the walls of our bedroom was against the roof, causing it to slope sharply to the floor. Toward that side, a short section of cast-iron vent pipe passed through to the roof from the bathroom. The window at the far end faced the southbound traffic on the road. I often lay awake at night watching the headlights create boxes of light against the far wall. The car came closer, the box grew brighter. Coming down the gentle slope towards the brook, the box dimmed slowly and started to close as the angle from the headlights sharpened. The light went from a box to a collapsing parallelogram; moving up at ever-increasing speed, it crossed onto the sloping ceiling, losing all hope of definition. The car sped by; the light shrank to nothingness as it flew toward the window.

The car rushed up the hill toward town. I was alone, abandoned.

One day a car will stop and someone with kindly authority, seeing my unbearable unhappiness and the wretched living conditions, will take me away to a happier home, with kind and accessible parents. Who could not want me? I am very nice, and I want to help around the place—I just don't want to be watched. My new father will help me stop wetting the bed, help me dress better, be less silly, do better in school, and stand between me and my new mother with a firm goodwill. We will go on vacations. Friends will come over and play and be happy and eat lots of snacks.

And I will be less invisible. Somewhere a screen door slaps spasmodically. The wind of the past is like the wind of the prairie: endless and absentminded and negligent. And the unruly crew of tumbleweeds with which it scours the ground: they start and stop and start again and run out and run in like sanderlings before an inrushing wave. A light bulb swings, its flat and uninterested light briefly relieves the dark, but never illuminates. A gate creaks, and again the wind urges along its scattered flock. Hither and thither they go, these flocks of tumbleweeds, which insistent and pitiless memory change into small, savage coils of concertina wire, and they roll over my naked and inconsequential body, and at last I can properly pay for all those failures: the failure of the hay bales, the failure of the tied-together string, and the failure of the circumcised triangle.

My parents' bedroom had no door, no lights, no heat (it had a register through the floor, but that opened into the library, itself usually unheated), and only the meanest of closets, the back of which was against the roof of the house and shared its abrupt angle; one knelt and pushed aside a sour-smelling curtain. A couple of chests of drawers, an old white wastebasket into which my mother would throw heavily bloodied tampons. Why should they fix the place up? They, kind of like Church Hill Road, were just on the way somewhere. It was a life in exile.

Chapter IV

The Kitchen

Muriel School Work, Kitchen, Augusta, 1955

Mommy correcting papers.

The kitchen—in effect our living room—bore a disproportionate share of everyone's waking hours. Under a naked florescent, the square wooden table in its center and its four scoop-bottomed chairs was the place of choice for snacks, homework, canning, clothes folding, dressmaking, coffee breaks, and marking papers. The kitchen was the first place to get warm on a winter morning, the only way to get to the bathroom, and the thoroughfare from the rest of the house to the back door. In the winter, my father lit the kerosene burners of the kitchen stove first and then tended to the furnace.

"Why didn't they leave the kerosene stove on low all night? I mean, Christ! the room was poorly insulated and had no cellar under it."

"Yeah, I know, then he could have just turned it up. Just cheap, I guess. That room could never be warm."

The banging of the furnace doors rumbled up into the house from the radiators and promised two things: eventual warmth and some degree of bad temper. Whether he could simply throw a log onto the still-glowing coals and open the damper for a few minutes or had to start cold with newspaper and kindling depended on how well the banked fire had lasted through the night. The last thing he did before going to bed was throw a large stick of wood into the furnace and close the damper as much as possible to make the fire burn more slowly. Whatever the condition in which he found it, the rest of the house was still freezing by the time we had to get up for school. I got dressed and had breakfast in a fug of cigarette smoke, coffee, and wet pajamas, syncopated by the necessary use of the bathroom and the surges of cold air consequent to the opening of the back door when someone needed to grab a coat or do the chores or start the car.

My mother used the kitchen as a dressing room, too, but this primarily revolved around the laborious process of putting on heavy, elastic stockings and hitching them up to a garter belt with its little rubbery knobs that get squeezed into the narrowing metal clip. On one leg this was preceded by applying a patch to the ulcer near her ankle, taping it on, and then easing the stocking over it. This patch was built up out of some generic foam. The rest of the stocking was stretched up over her vein-scarred leg. She then put on nylons to dull the artificiality of the elastic stockings, the vitality of whose color extended only as far as the advertising on the box in which they came.

"I could have had a dozen," she told me once when the subject of giving birth came up. She was simply revisiting a personal fiction—I suppose we all have them to keep us alive—but in her case it was to keep her from seeing that for her it might have been better to have had none.

In the evening, she ate sitting sideways between the table and the stove, her feet up on a kitchen stool—

too narrow, and a bit too tall, but making do was a virtue.

After supper and before washing dishes, sitting next to the warm stove, she allowed herself a nap. She folded her arms, and her head dropped down, and she slept for a few minutes. After the dishes, there was often work from school and papers to grade.

I woke her up once for some reason—some stupidity, I'm sure. Were there no other adults in the house who might have protected her nap or draped a shawl around her shoulders or started the dishes? Apparently not.

The stove dominated the kitchen by its size and by standing out into the room, as the center of the back wall was built out around a chimney. It squatted immovably on short, curved legs, its bulging oven door proudly proclaiming "Dual Atlantic" in porcelain-covered cast-iron letters arched over a non-working thermometer. To the right, the gas range, to the left of the oven were the kerosene burners. They heated the large, flat stovetop above them, a surface that could be used to make hot water or simmer soup, as long as you had time to wait.

"Hot water? Didn't you get hot water?"

"No. Just running cold water for the toilet and the bathtub, and after a number of years the kitchen sink. The pump finally went away."

"What'd you do, take cold baths?"

"No, we heated water on the kitchen stove in a big canning pot, poured it in, and tempered it with water from the faucet. Not great— the water level never approached luxury; in the winter, the hot water had to heat this heavy, cast-iron bathtub."

"Well, why'd you stick with the pump in the kitchen? Somebody had to pipe the water to the bathtub—why not to the kitchen at the same time? They were right next to each other."

"Because the kitchen had no cellar underneath it, running the pipe was clumsy and had to wait. And then, in the winter, there was the danger of a water pipe freezing in an unheated crawl space. That filthy, cold, space was also the reason the kitchen had no furnace ducts and so had to be heated by the kerosene stove."

"How did you get water to the bathroom? Did it come into the house by gravity?"

"No, they brought in a backhoe, trenched from the well to the house, ran pipe to the cellar, and then put in an electric pump."

Lids, flush with the top of the kitchen stove, gave entry to the burners: each lid had a notch in its rim to make it easy to remove. The burners, viewed from the top, looked like a series of four, evenly-spaced concentric cylinders, each about ten inches high. The inner ones were ventilated. At the base of each space sat the wick, inserted on its edge into a circular groove; each one had to be lit manually once it was saturated. As the burners needed it, they pulled in more fuel from the refillable, gravity-fed tank at the back of the stove. The tank's gentle "tunk, tunk, tunk" was a part of every winter day.

"How'd you get the kerosene to the stove?"

"An ugly chore. One lifted the small tank out of its reservoir behind the stove and headed outside. The kerosene barrels rested heavily on wooden racks by the back stoop. In the winter they collected ice and snow on top, so the first task was to remove this crown to avoid having snow fall into the tank, and the next to shovel a place for the tank to rest under the drum's nozzle while filling it. Remove the tank's small cover—"

"How small is small?"

"Two inches, maybe. Small enough so that, to avoid splashing, you had to have the strength to hold the tank up to the nozzle."

"Why'nt you just leave the cover inside?"

"Not that clever, I guess. Anyhow, since I didn't have the strength to hold the tank up to the nozzle of the drum, I had to line it up with the tank's opening and hope. But I always got some on the outside, and some on my hands, and the stuff smells ugly. Going inside, I had to make sure there was no snow stuck to the bottom to melt and make puddles—or worse, as the tank was inverted into the reservoir, the water from the melting snow might run down the side of the tank and so into the stove's fuel supply."

"Why do you remember this in such detail?"

"I tried to sail by it in a few sentences, but my editor pointed out that my compressed informality (a charitable description) assumed the reader knew the geography of that old house and which tank was inside and which tanks were outside. So I rewrote it."

And in the rewriting, I found the invoking of hope very troubling.

Hope is the universal sustainer of the invisible; here, in reality, a kind of mute desperation. Of what good was hope, when aligning the nozzle and the container required experience, luck and good depth perception? Luck I knew little of, depth perception I had none of, and my experience was that such an attempt always ended in a mess—

a corrosive paradigm of failure, repeatedly reinforced.

The insidious erosion of confidence and competence contained herein might have been easily reversed with a 50c funnel.

A high shelf against the broad back of the stove was supported at each end by filigreed ironwork, the manufacturer's one attempt to lighten the stove's grim utility. It was only a gesture. Behind, a large exposed flue went to the chimney.

Handy slept on a rug in a warm spot next to the stove. Handy was our dog, a beagle mutt, and was the last of an unexpected litter born in Center Montville.

"You remember the time he came back from being out all night all scratched and bitten up, barely able to drag himself whimpering to the house?"

"Yeah, he must of got into a terrible fight somewhere. Daddy took one look, carried him to the car, and tore off for the vet. Well, maybe not tore off—we never had cars that could tear anyplace—but driving as fast as he could. He later reported he ran red lights. Handy came home a few days later with large areas shaved and his wounds sutured with heavy staples with their points sticking out."

"Why do you suppose they did it that way?"

"To keep him from scratching those places, I think."

"What happened to him, anyway?"

"I don't remember. At some point he fades from the scene, and from memory."

When we first moved in, we had an icebox and had to go over to Leavitt's several times a week. Their general store was a few miles out on South Belfast Avenue. The ice house, a cavernous green building, deliciously cool and damp on a hot summer day, stood behind it. They dug out a large block of ice and muscled it onto a dolly with big ice tongs. Having hosed off the sawdust, one handle of the tongs served to hook the block to a large beam scale, as ice was sold by the pound. We hurried home.

The cats had the run of the place, sometimes snoozing on your lap, other times on a favorite chair. Most of our cats—Blackie, Schwenzil, Some-Fun—

since Daddy liked math and puns, why didn't he name it Sum-Fun?—

had long and off-putting pathologies; Taffy was more your normal, lazy cat and spent a large part of each winter under the kitchen stove.

Next to the stove stood the washing machine: on the bottom, an exposed electric motor, dust clinging to its dull, oily, blackness; above the motor, a big copper tub, a remarkable thing, with a lid of the same material, its ribbed flange sitting inside the tub's lip gave a tight fit. The removable agitator was also a remarkable thing: three shiny metal bowls hung plunger-like from three branches, the branches extending from a central shaft like wall sconces. While rotating the shaft slowly, the motor moved the agitator up and down sharply, creating tidal waves at each stroke, clobbering the clothes. Dirt, grime and manure ran from this torture as if possessed. When finished, the machine pumped the wash water into the sink via a hooked hose. All these phases required baby sitting: the machine knew nothing of automatic cycles or permanent press or spin drying. It had one setting: Total War. As we had no hot water in the house, my mother heated it on the stove in the same big pots in which we heated bath water. This she poured into the washing-machine tub, tempering it with cold from the pump. The machine ca-thunked its way through the washing cycle. More water went in for the rinse.

"She had to wring out the clothes by hand?"

"No, mounted at the back was a wringer, whose lip hung over the tub. A verticle shaft from the motor, its gears separately engaged by a lever, made the wringer turn. She took the clothes out of the tub and fed them one by one through the wringer, which had an emergency disengagement lever on top in case something was too thick, or you got your fingers in it."

"She then had to hang the laundry outside on the line?"

"Well, in the summer. But hanging the wash out on the line in the winter created certain difficulties when trying to fold it because it froze. Early on, my mother got a gas dryer, but there was no room for it in the kitchen, so the pleasure derived from having such a new appliance was diminished by having to put it deep in the unheated back hall."

Diagonally across from the washing machine was a black, cast-iron sink. Maybe twenty inches wide and eight inches deep, it sat on metal legs enclosed in primitive cabinetry. On one end of the sink was a small sideboard, on the other a tall hand-pump; above, a long shelf, a catch-all for often-needed things like toothbrushes, hairpins, shaving equipment, and false teeth, and above that a light fixture: a single bulb in one of those glass covers that look like reworked jelly jars. When anything in the kitchen had to be covered, linoleum was the material of choice; drying and wetting over the years caused that on the sideboard to heave like a country road in the winter.

To get water from a pump you have to have priming water, which, when poured down the pump's throat, swells the leather innards—the pump's equivalent of piston rings. Moving the handle causes the now-snug piston to move up and down, creating a vacuum; the leather flap-like diaphragm at the bottom closes on the piston's down-stroke to hold the vacuum which each upstroke increases, and the water comes up the pipe. We had an unspoken competition as to who could get water with the least amount of priming and the fewest strokes of the pump handle. Here small strokes worked better. To get water quickly, you had to produce a good vacuum; a good vacuum required imagination and a sense of touch, like a blind doctor performing a gynecological examination. Short, quick throws of the handle in just the right position, the vacuum, the snug piston, the wet leather flap of the valve opening and closing—and here's the water. We measured performance by how much water was left in the priming bucket. Whatever might be your need for getting water, the priming bucket was refilled first. I sometimes ran out.

In the corner beyond the washing machine, a little pantry was built into the wall: some shelves behind a pair of wretchedly fitting, glass-paned doors above and several crudely built drawers below. They were of the variety that, upon opening, canted down at such a steep angle that everything rolled to the front; open it a bit further and the drawer fell out. One side of the cupboard was against a poorly insulated outside wall, and the back was against the unheated back hall. Until we got an electric refrigerator, we used the cupboard during the winter as an ice box, but without having to buy ice. If we ever ran out of space in the cupboard, we had unheated rooms which on winter mornings were indistinguishable from walk-in refrigerators.

In the corner on the other side of the sink: cupboards top and bottom, with painted wooden doors. The doors were homemade and, although functional, devoid of either woodworking sophistication or decoration. Dishes and glasses up, pots and pans and baking utensils down. The top cupboard was raised, giving a small counter top on the bottom, and yes, it was covered with linoleum. Breadbox, toaster, mixer. Further along the same wall, the bathroom door, and next a tall, flimsy metal cabinet, so loose at the joints that a hard pull on the handle threatened to collapse the entire thing in a rhomboid jumble. This locker-like affair contained medicines, home-doctoring equipment on permanent loan from the Augusta State Hospital, neatly folded towels, and those always-troubling, naked, hypodermic syringes. It smelled of medicine and mystery: iodine, gentian-violet, Band-Aids, aspirin, Vicks. The doorway to the "living room"—more often the "don't sit in that room now" room, and off hours in the winter the "can't sit in that room anyway" room—was in the remaining corner of the kitchen.

On the wall opposite the sink, a desk of sorts, with a lamp, and maybe a short chest of drawers and a narrow, open-shelved bookcase with a closed cubby at the bottom—it contained strata of unclassifiable objects, saved, deposited, buried. Before getting to the door to the unheated back hall and the outside back door, a row of hooks for coats, and, in the winter, boots below. Leaving your boots outside in the hallway in the winter, while more virtuous, insured their thorough overnight refrigeration. The floor sloped a bit. White chintz curtains, homemade, a checkerboard floor of brown-and-cream linoleum tiles. The entire room gave the feeling of need and exposure and boniness.

Chapter V

The Barn

The barn had lost most of its floor some years before. The inside ends of the floor's planks sloped down from the sills, their rotten ends tapering into the dirt where we parked the car. What remained was badly grooved from years of wear. A heavy wooden door slid ponderously into a niche between the wall and a steep stairway to the second floor where we stored bales of straw and some of the seasonal equipment. The flanged steel wheels fixed at the top of the door ran along a metal bar, which, whether from some unfortunate collision with a vehicle or just from fatigue, was no longer straight. Moving the door elicited screeching protests, like a subway car negotiating a too-sharp curve.

For years the frost had heaved the rocks on which the barn's sills had originally rested. Solid footing gone, the barn sat on the ground in resigned old age. Though nothing was plumb, it still functioned, if only as a place to keep a bewildering array of tools, tire chains, pieces of garden hose, barrels, bicycles, steel cable, rope, scrap wood, chicken crates, kerosene lanterns, ice-cutting equipment, odd pieces of harness, cant dogs, an old scythe—everything in a frightening, cobwebby jumble.

A big roll-top desk stood to one side, on which and in which were an indescribable assortment of containers, holding, in various stages of rust and decay, at least one representative sample of every piece of hardware produced since the Great War. It was an article of faith that for any piece of hardware, x, there existed somewhere in some box or drawer another x. Behind this desk and scattered around the walls on nails were parts for machinery long since retired by the previous owners, parts of buildings long since destroyed, cans of gas, oil for the car, and oil for various machinery, oil for machinery we did not yet own, and old paint that when opened revealed a gelatinous mass of hardened pigment under a sloshing wash of vehicle.

Along the front wall opposite the stairs was a steel vise sitting mutely on a narrow workbench of heavy planks, its work surface eroded and cupped by decades of abuse. In the far corner were the barrels for the grain and the door to the duck house. The whole lower floor was lit by a single, dirty bulb in the back, whose switch was in a rough niche just inside the sliding door. Reaching a bare hand into its cobwebs and darkness required courage. If the bulb blew, you had to walk in with a flashlight, whose movement caused the machinery to project wildly shifting shadows on the walls, a bestiary of carnivorous monsters waiting to leap on you as soon as you leaned down into the feed barrel or otherwise turned your back.

Someone in more prosperous times had mounted a sign outside over the barn's sliding door: "Sunnybrook Farm" it proudly proclaimed. It had been painted over before we arrived, but you still could make out the name in slightly raised, ten-inch letters.

Chapter VI

The Duck House

Hugh. Duckhouse in back.

B eyond the barn and connected to it by a short passage was a long, low shed affectionately called the "duck house." It was divided into two parts, and each part had a small, low door which could be raised and latched open like the gun ports on a 74. Since waterfowl are one of nature's most productive manure engines, every weekend we had to shoo the residents out into the fenced-in yard and, with shovel, fork and hoe, clean the place, or as farm workers would say it, "we mucked out the ducks and geese." Having cleaned out the old, we spread the floor with fresh straw purchased just for this purpose. The new hay scratched my hands as I tore handfuls from the compressed bale—

loose please, no clumps—

and scattered it around. The air was full of dust and ragweed pollen, the ducks and geese quacked appreciatively, and the treads of my boots were full of duck shit.

However, Jeb and I learned a lot from my father. First, just exactly what was the best way to clean this duck house, and how might one do the best job with the fewest strokes? Do not think that this was merely a cleaning job—get the old stuff out the door, get the new stuff down. The topology of the duck-house floor was reviewed every time we cleaned it. Where were the nails sticking up that prevented you from using the clean sweep of the shovel? Where were the boards so warped you had to use the hoe? Such simple details acquired depth, and, because of his constant processing and reprocessing of the past, became abstracted in my father's eyes into pieces of some unfinished world. He was there and not there. And then there were the quotes and the songs: the culture of the world rolled across those old planks, dark with mire and overuse. "La donna e'mobile," "The Ballad of Sir Patrick Spens," Eliot, Dante, Baudelaire, Shakespeare, Joyce, Sean O'Casey, Frost, ballads and snatches of vaudeville songs. He said them for himself, seemingly; listeners were welcome, but to ask a question like, "What is that?" or "What does that mean?"—well, I always felt foolish. It would have been so much better if I had known that stuff already. But they weren't foolish

questions, just out of place, because his intended if unspoken message was that these things had value. He was not showing off. He was not in some way transferring knowledge to those listening; those things—that wide-ranging knowledge and appreciation—were his in a way that he could not give over. He was there and not there. He watched himself clean the duck house, as he watched himself live.

When young friends were around, these outbursts embarrassed me, and I assumed they figured my father was, well, strange.

And yet somewhere I knew he was not strange, that from some perspective Daddy knew everything worth knowing. But I could never figure out just where to stand. Never was there a kid who wanted more to be in both worlds and ended up in neither. But, like everything else he never taught me, I got even by learning it anyway. Allen Farnum came over a number of times one summer, and my mother helped him with his reading skills. He told me years later that he went home and exclaimed to his parents, "You should hear what those people talk about! They are so smart!" My parents knew so much and yet were invisible, as if they had made a suicide pact and only partially carried it out.

Part II

Spring

The midday sun mounts higher in the sky, now well along in its summer ecliptic, the air softens, and the land lumbers to its feet. The ground freezes every night, and the mornings are sharp with the smell of frost, but the cold has none of its earlier vice-like grip. Each morning, the ice on the puddles invites judicious testing with a toe. Pressure first produces radial faults, then transforms the clear, icy skin to milky opacity. Matted vegetation covers the fields; in the gardens only a few rows of blackened stalks remain. The soil is hard and sullen; the houses look tentative, relieved, no longer so brave.

Nature seems confused, stalled—restoring a sense of purpose to the land requires such an effort, such an effort. Where does one begin? Maybe this year we will skip this rebirth and lushness. We are tired—tired of the never-ending, Etesian cycles of little benefit. Yes, for a few months we put on a nice show, but it always seems a kind of manic desperation—next winter will again leave us soggy and short of breath.

The winter woods, the green of pines, the white of birches, and the grey of bare hardwoods pay little attention to such changes. Like the fur of a wild animal, the woods have depth and a certain melded complexity—nothing is of a single color.

Small shoots start to push through the matted grass, an intense green against the etiolated vegetation. The brook washes the last piece of ice over the dam. Pussy willows, those plainest of weeds, are greeted as the fulfillment of some promise, shared but unspoken; we treasure them. Crocuses explode from the tawny grass, reminding us that there is color in the world and, almost as if surprised at our own discovery, we have missed it. The frogs wake up and busy themselves laying millions of eggs, which in time turn into as many tadpoles. We always put some eggs in a jar in order to watch them grow, but they took too long, and our scientific zeal tapered off. Our parents dumped them long before they became frogs. The narcissus revive, last year's cattails nod at the edges of the brook, Queen Anne's lace returns to the ditches, coltsfoot to the fields. Grab some lamb's lettuce (officially, corn salad) or some wild chives without paying a great deal of attention to their provenance. Pull a leaf off milkweed and watch the "milk" run down the stem. And then the perennial fiddlehead fern discussions: everyone knows about them, but they seem always to be eaten by other people. This may be in part because you have to know *which* of the ferns are edible: *all* ferns go through a fiddlehead stage, but only several of them are edible. Big Vs of geese pass overhead, flying north, their bleating honks fill the air, their long journey touches our hearts. There is no one so dull as to fail to look.

They leave behind the mystery of a long journey, the ache of rootless wandering. Theirs is the ultimate freedom: they never have to arrive anywhere.

The land greens slowly. The trees start working on leaves: Memorial Day will find them just about finished. The imperative of renewal quickens—the age-old enthusiasm has returned, in spite of earlier philosophical doubts. Sorrel and smartweed and chickweed and pale yellow mustard and vervain, as yet without its purple spikes, stand in the ditches. Wild grapes blossom, gnarled old apple trees, even those in Mollison's ill-tended orchard, put on glorious crowns, brilliant white trillium trumpets under the oaks and maples of the old graveyard down Blair Road. In the fields are violets, clover and buttercups. And the robins are back.

Chapter VII

Hatching

The greater space and dignity we might have anticipated with the receding oppression of the winter was, for us, simply a mirage, for into our crowded kitchen were thrust, sometime toward the end of March, four incubators, each roughly half the size of a snooker table, but with rather more depth. My father cleverly left the long legs off two of them and, using a couple of pieces of two-by-four as spacers, stacked the legless on the legged. The warming weather convinced the dour waterfowl to embark on yet another reproductive adventure, and morning and evening we heartlessly snatched these potential Thanksgiving dinners from their still-warm nests. For a duck, only a full nest hits the instinctual "stop-laying" button, and since their nests were never full, the eggs never stopped. We had eggs, many eggs. They went immediately into one of the electric mothers, whose constancy and warmth, while admirable, failed to make up for certain shortcomings in their parenting skills. The ducks got the big incubator in the cellar; the geese, being somewhat the rarer animal, got the kitchen.

Each of the kitchen incubators had two shallow wooden drawers, side by side, behind dropdown, glass-front doors. The bottom of each drawer was of heavy wire mesh. Resting on this was a moveable, panel-like contraption of heavy wire which rode in dadoed slots in the drawer's wooden frame. Its wires undulated across the drawer in symmetric counterpoint, each wire bay intended to hold one egg. The wire bay did more than keep its awkwardly spheroid parcel from some careening misadventure; it was an important part of the designer's attempt to mimic the actions of an attentive, web-footed mother, for attached to this wire panel was a handle, and by sliding the handle a full throw, the wire cradles rolled their awkward loads 180 degrees, thus preventing the developing embryo from sticking to one side of the shell or hatching with birth defects.

But how could a mere mechanical device replace the tender attention of the mother bird as she uses her bill to turn the eggs in her nest? Couldn't, of course. And these mechanisms were deemed unreliable, in part because they were designed for eggs with a smaller girth than a goose egg. So we turned the eggs by hand, individually rotating them once a day—such care, such attention, that could be neither bought nor hired. For in this sea of large, polished stones, each looked so much like its neighbor that only love could keep track of which ones had been turned. Let your attention drift for a moment, and you return hopelessly confused.

"Why didn't you just mark them to reduce the confusion?"
"We never seemed to have figured out . . ."

Then there was the sprinkling. When the mother bird left the nest for one of her short breaks—breaks spent swimming in the nearby pond in search of something to eat—the exposed eggs had a chance to cool. Instinctively, before coming back, she flapped and splashed in the water to get as wet as possible; back on the nest, she shook her body, and a tiny rainstorm moistened the eggs, the evaporating water further cooling these furnaces of developing life. In imitation of this, one at a time the heavy drawers came out of the incubator and were placed on the cast-iron sink. When just warm to the touch, we sprinkled them using a beer bottle with a big, corked sprinkler head on it; back they went to their mechanical mother, none the wiser that their real mother had not fussed over them. Three times a day this parallel of the natural world got reenacted.

"What a pain! What else did you have to do by hand?"
"In the third week, about halfway through the hatching cycle, we had to candle the eggs."
"With a candle? Is that how it got its name?"
"Yes, but we used electricity."

A candler looks like a trouble light with the bulb, except for a small opening, completely enclosed. The concentration of the light is such that when the opening is held against an egg in a darkened room, it reveals the air space and the developing network of blood vessels signaling a viable embryo. The eggs that failed the test were weeded out with the simple matter-of-factness common to farmers and which was displayed, without passion, anytime a creature was not wanted or could not keep up with its peers.

In anticipation of birth day, yet more equipment came into the kitchen: the brooders. We had two of them—ugly, squat, utilitarian affairs of galvanized steel and wire mesh. They sat on top of the incubators. Troughs at the sides for water and grain; a low-roofed shelter area in the back, heated; trays underneath which we lined with the winter's newspapers to keep things neat. Around day twenty-seven, the pipping started. The gosling, limbs tortuously bent and entwined and filling its confining home to the point of near immobility, used a sharp, chisel-like protrusion on the end of the bill to wear a hole through the shell. Resting often during this awkward, exhausting effort, it widened the hole until finally the shell, worn thin during the incubation, broke apart, leaving the tiny bird, down matted with albumen, struggling to straighten its limbs and stand upright. In the several days that followed, the tray became a mass of tiny, peeping creatures in various stages of the struggle. There were always some assisted births: "Here, let me extend that crack a little." For a few, even such tender midwifery failed; the wracking effort to get out was too much.

Some short time after it could sit up, this fragile creature, covered with yellow fuzz of little more substance than lint, joined the other ducklings and goslings in the brooder. Soon it attempted its first, lurching steps to get to the water trough. Mash, a vile-looking slop of ground grain and water, followed. In a few days, we changed to the junior, pelletized version of this mash, to everyone's relief—it was dry, easier to handle, and most particularly, easier to clean up. Soon we added lettuce scraps to their diet. They grew apace, still oh-so-cute, but getting noisier and smellier daily. Finally, now a big handful and hardened to some of the rigors of waterfowl life, they got promoted to the barn and the big circular brooders. This was always a moment of tender anxiety, since the nights, particularly, were yet far from warm, the larger birds hogged the feeding troughs (we pushed them away in an effort to level the field), and all huddled in a solid mass of bodies at night, the bigger birds might smother the smaller. Thunder, equipment failures, predators, more ducklings and goslings on the way: we needed the current residents to quickly gain waterfowl street smarts. And so the cycle repeated itself—1,400 ducklings, 600 goslings. By the end, the pile of saved newspapers was getting dangerously low. Some birds were sold to farmers and people who wanted to grow their own meat, but the more usual sale was two or three to someone who had a camp on a lake and wanted to raise them as pets.

Birds born with birth defects were destroyed. They would not grow normally. They could not compete for food. They were slow and easy prey for predators. One year, a duckling with a turned-in foot made it through the selection process. It moved lurchingly, since the leg with the bad foot collapsed at every step. We made a pet of it; it ate out of our hand; we carried it on waterfowl forced marches from one field to another. He made it to early adulthood. One day my father, seeing in Gimpy's heaving walk the terrible consequences of his original mercy, or maybe he was just annoyed, took an axe and chopped off its head.

Years later I met a woman who had a pet calf named Lucky. One day she came home and didn't find it: on asking, she found out that it was in the freezer. She will carry that damage to the grave.

In response to the fresh air and bags of grain, the hundreds of unsold ducklings and goslings grew apace, and Lo! the land was full of them. You have to be careful with birds—overcrowding will produce antisocial behavior. Much as a hardened commuter will casually bump someone with his briefcase, someone who has flaunted the rules of close living, say, by cutting the escalator line—all the while innocently staring off into space as if noticing for the first time that the walls and ceiling meet at right angles—so will crowded birds casually peck each other in passing until an ugly bleeding sore appears on the back of the wing. Give them more room, and this behavior vanishes nearly overnight.

Cannibalism was serious but rare, as they had the run of the place, except for the occasional hoarding to keep them off the lawn or the road and out of the garden. One of our favorite fencing materials was unfolded vegetable crates. On the way home from a shopping trip, my father stopped at different supermarkets, went in the back, and asked the produce man for the cast-offs from the lettuce and cabbage or whatever else they might have. These he carried out and put in the car, so we frequently carried home crates of unsalable, partially rotten greens. Other kids had fathers who brought home the bacon; mine brought home the garbage.

Chapter VIII

Mommy Gets Sick

In May of 1950 my mother got sick. I was too young to understand the progression of illness: one day she was walking, the next day she was in a rented hospital bed in the living room, unable to walk, barely able to move her hands. There was no diagnosis—some sort of myelitis. Years later I met someone who, depressed over the loss of his community and consequently his pulpit, developed the same symptoms and managed the same recovery. I now know she had Guillain-Barré syndrome, a disorder where the immune system attacks the sheaths of the nerves. There are no known causes: a viral or an upper respiratory illness often precedes it, or maybe exposure to tuberculosis. She had had bouts of pleurisy and bronchitis. She was then teaching in Chelsea in a dirt-poor, one-room schoolhouse, with a privy and a woodstove. She sold snacks to those who could afford them and used the profits to buy school supplies.

My father seemed never around. He was working at the Augusta State Hospital. Her condition and possible loss must have made him nearly mad. Even several years later and

Augusta, 1952

Muriel alone, back door, Augusta.

now healthy, when she about to go to Florida for two weeks to see her mother, he developed symptoms of a heart attack.

I remember him carrying her out to the car, a 1938 Oldsmobile Coupe with just enough room in the back seat for kids. The seats were fuzzy and smelled of dust, and the side windows did not roll down. We were on our way to the doctor. The memories are indistinct, like two others that I asked my parents about years later: one was that of riding in the cab of a truck, a moving van, with my brother and my mother. The other was of riding in the caboose of a train that had a coal fire in a potbellied stove in the center, some sort of dark compartments at one end and several sacks of mail.

I asked how it was that we were riding in the caboose of a train. They gave some explanation—I don't remember their reply—but it was only an explanation: they had no answers for their lives. Much later I realized that their lives were their answers.

I had to help her with a bedpan, an ugly job for a seven-year-old, an uglier job for a seven-year-old boy. Bea Stevens, a woman from the neighborhood, came to help and cook. Her meals have faded, but I remember the value of her presence.

My father later described her as a "half-demented, part-Indian, alcoholic thief." Nothing silver in the house survived her visits—even the silver head of a cane.

By the end of that summer, we were looking very neglected. A

Archery set from Herbie Hollander. Augusta, 1950

friend of my father's from City College, Herbie Hollander, came for a visit.

They had made a trip to California together in 1934.

He brought a red Radio Flyer wagon, with the wooden sides that fit into external brackets, and an archery set with a hardboard target on an easel and suction-cup arrows. How I loved that archery set! The wagon, for years afterward, was pressed into service as a heavy-duty hand-truck, carrying improbable loads around the farm, particularly crates of ducks and geese going to the slaughterhouse. That the wheels stayed on produces the need for a trite aphorism, like, "They don't make 'em like that anymore."

Years later I remembered enjoying the spray of a hot shower at some undetermined point in my past but could not place the circumstances under which this might have happened. We never had a shower—we never had running hot water.

My mother was over sixty before she had running hot water in her own home.

And yet the reality of the shower was undeniable. On further consideration, the memory turned out to be another facet of Herbie's visit! He took us to his motel room for a hot shower and then to the barbershop to get a much-needed, store-bought haircut. Heaven's promise holds little approaching that afternoon. No relative of my mother's came to the house. A cousin, not just any cousin but a cousin with whom my father was close, came for a visit several summers later, but it was fifty years before she learned of my mother's paralysis.

I remember going to someone's house, possibly a parent from her school, and getting some toys and puzzles at Christmastime. I also got some hand-me-down clothes, among them a brown suit of which I was terribly proud. I wore it to school several times in my official capacity as treasurer of the Second Grade Club.

Can you imagine her lying there, day after day, night after night, with no entertainment beside the drivel from some local radio station, unable to get to the bathroom or take care of herself? And endlessly revisiting the past and the bitter irony of wasted effort and unfulfilled promise: Phi Beta Kappa in her junior year at the University of Chicago and an aid to President Hutchins. A BA in philosophy and master's degrees in both piano and composition. A scholarship to study with Nadia Boulanger at the Paris Conservatory. Talent unvalidated by her pedestrian, bourgeois

Muriel and graduation group.

family, cut off from it by her mother, who herself had been cut off for marrying the wrong man but who was so lacking in empathy as to have learned nothing from the experience—to die in a house without a sink with running water. And yet to survive. Let others weep over the bravery of Hester Prynne for returning home, or maintain that you don't know bravery until you know Starbuck, in whose name Melville sums it up in four or five lines. I have a more immediate model.

The specialists could do nothing. A transplant from Texas, Dr. Mollison lived up the hill and worked at the local VA hospital. He came to the house repeatedly, encouraging her to try again and to try yet again to flex the knee of one leg. She finally did it. Then the other leg. By March of the following year, she was walking—maybe even back at that wretched school to finish the year. She recovered fully. The following fall, she got a job teaching in a consolidated public school in Vassalboro. Her illness became invisible. She never spoke of the episode again.

Chapter IX

Marbles

Y ou guys play marbles in the spring?"

"Sure, but not the way you've seen in those nostalgic pictures of boys in knickers trying to knock others' marbles out of the circle."

"So how did you play?"

"There were a couple of different ways. But marble games slog along predictably: no romance, no conflict, no sex—and so the story becomes quickly boring. Let's talk about something else."

"Wait, wait! how did your brother get all those cans of marbles—you remember, the ones up in the attic?"

"Oh, that's easy. He was teased because of his goofy looks, his glasses, and his extreme precociousness, so he got even with his tormentors by taking all their marbles. He had more marbles than God."

The game required some of the same skills as playing poker. You secretly enclosed a number of marbles in your hand, held out your closed fist to your opponent, and challenged, "How many?" If your opponent guessed wrong, he gave you as many marbles as you *did* have in your hand, and you went again; if he guessed right, your marbles were forfeit, and the challenge passed to him. The more marbles you could hold in your hand the better, without of course the mass of them forcing open spaces between your fingers or otherwise signaling that you had a handful of marbles and not a handful of air. For a cagey player, guessing was easier than you might think. One or two marbles were only used for bluffing and avoiding any hint of a pattern, since the gain or loss was not significant. After several turns, you could figure out the maximum number of marbles your opponent could hold in his hand and keep his fingers closed. Five or six maybe. Seven, and there were spaces between the fingers, or the pinky would not close, or the knuckles were white from the pressure. So the most common number was between three and six. There were any number of signals of more marbles: tone of voice, aggressive presentation, taking too long getting the marbles secretly into the hand. I missed them all, even the blatant ones like how far the fingernails were dug into the opposing flesh. Jeremy was very shrewd and missed nothing. And in this guessing game, he was the Prince of Darkness.

"I don't get it. How could you see anything from a fist thrust at you knuckles-up?"

"Allowing or disallowing certain things that aided the guesser were agreed upon before the game began. 'No turnsies' meant that you could not turn your opponent's hand over after he presented it knuckles up, while 'no feelsies' meant that you could not palpate your opponent's fingers for signs of sponginess, indicating a handful of mostly air."

"And how did you do?"

"Not very well, like I said. I mostly played the other marble game: the one in the dirt."

"You played that one during the winter?"

"No, you had to wait until the frost was out of the ground."

The area immediately around the part of the school where these games flourished was of uneven terrain, unsullied by grass or shrubs and composed of dirt and gravel with embedded rocks, tramped hard by countless feet. But all you needed was a patch of reasonably dry dirt; sometimes, in our enthusiasm, we waived even that requirement. A hole of a certain dimension was dug with your heel, either in the open or against a wall. Starting from some distant, agreed-upon point, you attempted to get your "shooter" marble into the pot in less turns than your opponent. As the players alternated, the shooters were moved closer and closer to the pot until one of them went in, and the others did not. Long shots sometimes worked, but the chance of hitting a rock sticking out at an oblique angle and thus having your shooter carom off into some even-more-inhospitable area was reason to consider this strategy carefully. The loser's (more than one could play) marble was forfeit, and since each player had put an equal number of marbles into the pot, the winner got all the marbles.

Like the other game, certain rules were agreed to before play started: "no changies" meant that the loser could not exchange his shooter for another marble, a serious loss if you happened to be lucky enough to have, instead of a marble, a ball bearing.

No "picksies" meant you had to make your shots roll along the ground, rather than using a hooked finger as a "nine-iron" to leap obstacles thrust up in your way like small Matterhorns; "no roundsies" and "no squarsies" prohibited you from taking your shooter out of the rough, say a mud puddle, and while inscribing either an arc or some part of an irregular rectangle in the dirt, moving it to a point of advantage at the same distance from the pot. The application of these rules led to no end of arguments.

No tools were available to make the pot, and before a game we paid little attention to details like making sharp edges and thus making a clear distinction between pot and non-pot. More heated arguments ensued as to whether a shooter was in or not in, for it might exist in two places at once, like subatomic particles. Reshaping the pot provided little lasting satisfaction, since the new pot suffered from the same imprecision as the old, only with a greater diameter.

"What happened if the game was tied?"
"Played over."

Chapter X

The Avocados and the Two A&Ps

There were two A&Ps in town in those days, a big one across the river and a little one on Bangor Street closer to home. Any errand in town took you past the smaller; the larger was a special trip. The big one controlled all the inventory, sending on some part of each delivery as experience and shelf space dictated. The big one got the fruit and vegetable deliveries, and among them were avocados. As these got riper, the price dropped, but not enough to clear the inventory since the big store inevitably got more than its clientele of somewhat limited sophistication and less wealth was inclined to purchase. In order that the fruit not rot on his watch, the produce manager would pack up what didn't sell and send it across the river, where the small A&P dutifully put the avocados out for sale. Nobody bought at seventy-five cents; nobody bought at fifty cents. The fruit was now a turbid green, the color of dark seaweed, and when squeezed appeared to be filled with wallpaper paste. Nobody bought the rotten fruit. The price finally went to four for a dollar. My parents bought them all.

Chapter XI

Meals

Meals were painful. There was the Daddy Bear, the Mommy Bear, the Oh-So-Clever Bear, and the You-Should-Have-Been-A-Girl Bear, known herein as Foolish Bear. We sat down at 6 p.m. with the Yankee Network News Service on WRDO; 6:05 was tolerable; 6:10 elicited some ill-tempered remark from Daddy Bear about the inadequacy of the service. The Daddy Bear lunged at his food as if it was going to be snatched away any second; he sometimes bit his own flesh, which produced a cry of pain. Mommy Bear would look at Daddy Bear and give him some minor words of comfort in a low voice; Oh-So-Clever Bear would sniff and seize the opportunity for some fatuously superior remark. Foolish Bear felt bad for Daddy Bear and worse for having to sit there; he used these interludes of pain to carefully review the architectural details of the kitchen table. Smarting, it was a while before Daddy Bear shifted back into high gear with the remaining food. Daddy Bear often barked out a sort of counterpoint to the news commentator, demolishing the announcer's analysis of international events with the Left's swift sword of righteousness, particularly when the news peddled thinly veiled, capitalist, self-interest as national policy. Yet, as dismissive as he might be of the bland radio fare, talking during the news invited an annoyed command for silence. As for any further conversation (there hadn't really been any yet), it was much subdued. Lame ol' Foolish Bear laid low and let the more clever bears carry on. Where's the dessert?

Foolish Bear was as a tolerated son-in-law, one whom the wife's parents accepted reluctantly, ever wishing their daughter had had the sense to choose better. Not a bad person, you understand: makes a living, spends too much money on haircuts, fails to use the obvious coupons in the grocery store, likes to get a chance to gently correct someone struggling to pronounce a word like "desuetude," dreams of sailing with Captain Jack

Aubrey on his daring adventures, and, like Jim before he jumped, is always prepared to sacrifice himself for the public validation of his unrecognized greatness.

Sometimes we were lucky enough to have steak. Our favorite cuts required marinating, a lot of marinating. Steak brought out Daddy Bear's relentless gastronomic dominance. Having gnawed every morsel off his own steak bones, he raised his head and looked around the table at ours to see if any displayed inadequate levels of mastication. In an instant he might snatch them from your plate and set upon them noisily; if not immediately forthcoming he broke them. Corn cobs on which you left some straggling kernels were also revisited. We had more corn in the garden, but that was not the issue. He was one of the few people ever to develop occlusion problems with dentures.

Part III

Summer

The fields of early summer are soft and inviting, stippled with color: countless wildflowers, some alone, some in big splashes; the red-orange flame of devil's paintbrush, clover, daisies, Queen Anne's lace, black-eyed Susans, buttercups, yarrow. Walking through them on such a day is to explore the world unburdened, a world relieved of all purpose except to exist.

Certain flowers conferred a special status on the finder: a lady slipper, softly pink and engorged and casually erotic, or maybe fringed gentian late in the summer, or maybe flags, with their ethereal, intense purple, or maybe under the pines near the brook a Jack-in-the-pulpit. The latter is a most remarkable plant, having a tall, straight flower stem, sensually inserted into a deep and softly contoured base. Wide green leaves surround it, green leaves with pronounced white stripes, while one from the back drapes over the spadix like a buggy tilt.

Nature's colors are like that, so pure that to imagine a color more intense requires your very soul to melt. In the imagining you come undone, transcendent. For at the instant it is first seen, a lady slipper justifies an entire universe created just for that moment. Yet, in the entire universe, who is there to see it but ourselves? Who else will weep? Despite of our tears, it nods carelessly in the breeze, as if mocking its own beauty, part of some strange order of existence whose reason for being ever remains a mystery. The freckled day lilies stretch open their orange arms like young girls in some innocent land, exposed, exuberant, unashamed. They do not seem to care that no one is mindful of their enthusiasm. Though they bloom for one day only, on that day they are everything they can be. They are beyond self-pity.

Summer came in stages. Sunny days in May were pleasant, but the evenings were cold; on Memorial Day, the slab of ice under the north side of the barn was, like a glacier, still retreating. Slipping off a rock while crossing the brook filled your sneakers with icy water. June brought the first hot days, but the evenings couldn't make up their minds what season they thought it was. June was when the final generation of fledglings moved out of the kitchen and into the barn. We cleaned up the incubators and associated junk and packed them away upstairs in the barn for the year. What a relief! The kitchen regained its former glory; it felt grand, open. Visits by friends were again possible. School ended at last: during its final days, kids breathlessly boasted of their plans for endless fun or their schemes to amass amazing private wealth.

Chapter XII

Nothing to Do

July brought the great exploring days. A great day started early, early enough so the grass was still wet. Great days were very rare; in fact they only happened when we had company, or a friend invited me to go to Webber Pond for the day. Even if there was no haying that day, there were chores and piano practice and probably some interminable project where I was in charge of standing around trying to look helpful, and my room to clean and the edges of the lawn to be clipped. Most of our lawn was edges, particularly while we still had the push mower. We had a sickle; it was, however, so dull it only beat down the grass. Our frustratingly dull shears were no more effective than baby scissors. Most times, I couldn't get free of these annoyances until after lunch. And even then I heard, offstage, remarks like:

From across the road, Augusta.

You haven't applied yourself to any heroic quests today.
You are not quite ready to play at Carnegie Hall.
You didn't vacuum the car.
Your pronunciation of French is not very good.

These delivered in a kind, patient voice. Whenever it was, I always cleared out of there with near-bursting lungs. Ditch all this nonsense—let Jeb handle the details—off on my own or off to a friend.

On uncaring days, we picked clover and pulled out the little flowers and ate the ends. Timothy, a tall grass with a large head like wheat, grew all over. We pulled out the top section to nibble on its tender end: it squeaked in complaint as it slid out of its damp, lower shaft; later in the summer it was too dry and the stem broke rather than slide out. Down low, bluets grew in patches, the airiest blue imaginable; singly, they would have been invisible, overpowered by their gaudier neighbors.

Lying down and shouting through opposite ends of a ten-inch culvert was fun. If I could have come up with something clever to shout, clever and vulgar, it could have been even more fun. The culvert under the road through which the brook flowed was so big we could walk through it—well, you had to scooch some—the spillway roaring, our voices echoing, the cobwebs sticking in our hair. Once through, we stood on the spillway with sticks and tried to stir up the bloodsuckers behind the dam. The now-exposed edges of the brook were muddy: maybe we could find some interesting junk thrown in there years ago? The mud sucked at the bottom of our sneakers. Water striders raced across the surface, each foot making tiny dimples in the water. Dragonflies zoomed around, making orthogonal turns and doing improbable aerial stunts like flying backwards. No sense in catching them: their iridescence fades completely in death.

"I didn't know they didn't keep their color."
"I got that from an entomology person. They are very cool, aren't they? They can fly thirty-five mph, flap the back wings down at the same moment they flap the forward wings up, and accelerate at four Gs."
"Yeah, cool, and old. Been around for 300,000,000 years!"

Flipping over a board uncovered a whole menagerie: the slugs and cocoons stayed attached; earthworms desperately wheeled into the ground; centipedes ran valiantly, but their acceleration was poor; grey sow bugs and ground beetles and rove beetles scattered in every direction.

A green snake slithered out of the grass: catching it was the high point of the day. Break off cattails, fence with them until the stems are broken, then pick apart the big, brown top. Pull on a floating water lily anchored to the bottom on a long stem—try to reach one with a white flower, beautiful but with a pungent smell. Pickerel weed grew along the edge of our brook—kind of neat, with its big glossy leaves and purple spikes of flowers. Once in a while we saw a blue heron standing in the water looking for food. It's tough to get a blue heron to smile, and a bike horn is an improvement over their hoarse, croaking call.

Across the road under the pines, things were quieter. The brook slowed, splashing gently and making pools. A woodpecker hammered. We kicked rotten stumps apart and watched the carpenter ants race out or used a stick to dig into piles of frass. Toadstools grew on trees, both the living and the dead: single ones, ferruginous, as big as salad plates, stepping up the side of a trunk; others, like a rash of dried, white apricots, scattered over a rotting stump; still others like bursts of small, yellow butterflies, marshaled high up. How generous is this world, giving space and uniqueness to so much variety! We poked at the conks in a dilatory way or broke them off, never bothering to learn more. Mushrooms we left alone, while assuring anyone listening that the one we just found, say, a particularly fine specimen that looked like a walnut-stained drawer pull on cheap furniture, was edible. We never tested our opinions.

We peeled pieces of bark off white birches and imagined a completed birch-bark canoe or broke the bark off an oak to expose the bark beetles' network of tunnels. Disease caused galls on some trees—big "sores" that exposed the inside layer of the tree and raised a thick, ugly welt around the edges.

Soft, red pasture roses grew along the stone walls—they had thorns but no smell. We broke off pieces of trees and smelled the fresh wood: alder, poplar, pine, spruce, willow. If you had a knife you could peel the willow and expose the smooth, ivory-green wood, slightly slick with sap.

Along the road, morning glories, with their big white trumpets and leaves shaped like heraldry shields, climbed high in the thickets and over the fences. And later on, bursts of tiny blue-black elderberries and bright-red chokecherries appeared. We always sampled them at least once every summer: maybe nature had taken a hint and made the fruit edible. They were awful, as were the small, very green apples grabbed from branches near the road. We grabbed a pine cone and walked along, methodically breaking off the scales. Hackmatack conelets are actually the best for this—there are fewer scales, and they are nicely spaced apart. Walking by a plant or a tree, we idly tore off leaves or buds or flowers and pulled them apart as if trying to learn something. We picked up, we examined, we threw down.

In the ditches made dusty by the passing traffic we stripped the tops off ragweed and Indian tobacco and the tan flowers off wild parsnip—the stem never broke, no matter how hard you pulled. You can't break the stem on an everlasting, either—pull hard enough and you uproot the whole plant. Queen Ann's lace smelled funny. Farmers don't like it—say it flavors the milk. Sorrel smelled like vinegar when you rubbed it between your fingers. We interrogated the columbine, turning up their crimson-horned lanterns and looking at the tiny yellow flames. Jimsonweed grew along the south side of Ernest's barn—leave it alone, it's poison, pretty white flowers or no. Mullien grew in places of little consequence or where foot traffic left only dirt. Its much larger cousin was a big, coarse, ugly nuisance, with palm-like leaves and long, subulating flowers waving in the air. Elsewhere I looked for rhubarb but found only horseradish. Burrs stuck on our pants and socks and even our shoelaces, their barbs making the pesky things difficult to pick off.

"God! This is so boring. You just wandering around and droning on about it! Who cares?"

"That's just it, I didn't care."

"You didn't care? What'd you do it for?"

"To get away. The wandering, the passiveness of it, the hopelessness of it, was a desperate if impossible flight to sexual neutrality, where if I could not be a boy at least I was not a girl, where if I could not be a writer, a machinist, or a boxer, at least I was not a musician—where I floated in a humid haze of uncertainty that shorted out every sense of direction, of accomplishment, and of hope, and since nothing had been accomplished, I could safely come home without that arrival being in some sense a challenge."

"How do you mean 'a challenge'"?

"My parents, in their own eyes, were failures, and I understood that to boast of some great accomplishment would be an assault on their fragility. I thus, in my hypersensitivity, managed to stay away from the real conflict, from home, and again—as with the women I have loved and failed, have let go, have walked away from—in the very essence of maleness, I failed to stand my ground, to stay at home, to fight like Leland did—"

"Who was Leland?"

"Leland Stamper in *Sometimes a Great Notion*. Finally fought his big brother to a standstill on the banks of the river. You saw the movie, I suppose?"

"Yes. Good movie."

"Nowhere near as good as the book: Viv, the woman they both love, is going away, in the rain, the interminable rain of the Oregon coast, and she uses her sleeve to wipe away the fog from the bus window and sees the tug towing the log booms down the river and Leland and Hank wearing calks—"

"What are calks?"

"Spiked boots with steel safety toes—dancing from log to log with their long peaveys, keeping the logs within their chains, each boom, amorphous, unruly, chained to the next like unevenly strung beads, headed to the Wakonda Pacific sawmill. Viv is leaving—she cannot mediate between the two men, now eternally locked in barely submerged conflict."

After the haying, the fields lie exposed, the harsh stubble crunching at every step. Each crunch stampedes small hordes of leaping grasshoppers. We catch them, and they exude some sort of brown juice on our hands which we call "molasses"—I don't think I want to know more.

We had to watch out for yellow jacket nests in the ground: they were a most unfriendly lot. And crossing pastures you needed to avoid the cow flops, at least the recent ones. The old ones were all dry, and you could step on them with impunity. Once in a while we saw a football-size wasp nest hanging off a limb. They have soft lines—not quite symmetrical—and look like they are made of feathery, grey paper. We knocked them down, but never in the summer, waiting rather until the weather got cold and all the hornets were napping.

We killed a couple of porcupines once, cut off their noses and two feet and took them to the town clerk to claim the bounty—fifty cents each. The clerk was none too excited about looking at the evidence. We made slingshots, hacking down some large bush to harvest the crotches, then attempting to cut a straight strip from an old inner tube, and finally tying it to each end of the Y with a crude knot. We didn't care that the elastics, cut from such a round, flexible shape, inevitably exhibited some of the unruliness of cooking bacon. And we made the other kind, too: a rock tied on the end of a piece of string whirled round and round and then released. If you were lucky it wrapped around a power line. Tin-can phones: make a small hole in the bottom of two cans and thread a strong piece of twine through both of them and make some sort of stopper knot. With a friend at the other end, stretch the string tightly, and shout—shout loudly enough and your friend could hear you easily.

In August, the frowsy sumacs along the road produced cones of fuzzy red berries, as well as loud assertions that the tree and everything on it was poison and that so-and-so had barely escaped death by touching it. Actually, it was harmless. It was the other sumac that was poisonous. We sat on the high ledges among the patches of tinder-dry saxifrage. Sulfurs and cabbage whites flitted through the garden. The bright sun drew out the heavy scent of the junipers, a plant we wanted to make more of but never could quite figure out how, other than biting the berries to get that sharp zing.

Chickadees, sparrows, robins with their orange-red breasts, and crows were so common as to elicit no comment. Ravens are indistinguishable from crows, except their call is less melodious, approximating a machine driving pilings. A hawk wheeling up high was a big thrill. Once in a while we might see an oriole with its bright orange breast, but birds like yellow warbles or cedar waxwings or hummingbirds were always seen when no one else was around, or a grownup saw one and we looked just a moment too late, which in the retelling was as good as actually having seen one.

On several occasions, we trudged deep into the woods toward the source of our brook, which some neighborhood kids claimed to have found. I never got further than the beaver dam with the pool backed up behind it. The beaver house was a big pile of sticks—the inhabitants had apparently left for more impressive digs.

Moving water always has mystery: What did it see on the way here? Where is it going? I tried to hear its messages. But though they were never quite revealed to me, I was sure they were there, and I was sure my father knew them—knew them all. And why did I want to know them? I wanted to write them down.

The logging roads, now green with disuse, went back several miles. The old loggers' cabins were wrecks, homes for birds, and full of animal droppings. Being so far away from home produced a kind of thrill, at least until a noise off in the woods reminded me of how far from home I actually was. Never saw much: squirrels, chipmunks, an occasional rabbit, woodchucks—nothing really exciting like Olivia Creelman who saw two bear cubs out behind her house, and Donny's father shot a bobcat. My father shot raccoons and skunks. Once a fox came too near the house— probably rabid or sick, causing it to lose all fear of humans. Jeremy or I had to bury these animals, their bodies heavy and rigid in death. A dead animal produces a sense of loss and, despite death, instinctual fear. The hole had to be deep, or some other animal might come at night and dig up a snack.

More exciting was going in the opposite direction—over toward the old granite quarries. We let ourselves down one giant step at a time, trying to avoid the poison ivy. Little seeps came out from rusty cracks in the walls. The quarries would have been more fun if they had water in them instead of so many rusty beer cans. On a hot day, it was nice to buy sodas at Renee's and drink them down in the quarry, sitting in the shade with our backs against the cool rock, feeling the long, smooth holes drilled to neatly split off giant blocks, blocks whose fractured edges were still sharp after a century. We met kids we didn't know there sometimes. If they were there first, I was too unsure of myself to barge in. We went to a different quarry. Once a big kid who was there with a girl told us to get lost. The girl laughed in an embarrassed way.

Playing on the railroad tracks or crossing them and going down to the edge of the Kennebec River was the best, but I never went. Some kids walked into town along the tracks. If asked by a parent, you never even heard of the Kennebec River. Once or twice every summer I went into town with Olivia and Jamie and a few others; we walked down to Riverside Drive and got on the Greyhound bus—twenty-five cents. Otherwise, I only got into town if my parents were going and decided, reluctantly, that they would leave me to wander around. Turn the corner, I'm out of sight, free at last! To enhance your chances of approval for such a waste of time, have a worthwhile activity to go to:

They're teaching origami at the Y this morning!

I want to go to the library and find out more about the Spanish Inquisition!

I'm going to meet Billy at Fort Western (dusty, dim, and historical) and then his brother said we could work in the booth with him at the Western Avenue street fair!

We ran after butterflies: monarchs, sulfurs, cabbage whites. Usually they evaded us. Rob Bridges had a net and a book and a whole collection all pinned and labeled. He could tell the difference between a monarch and a viceroy. He even had a black swallowtail. We? We just grabbed them with our hands. I guess they died, since our rough handling disturbed the dust on their wings.

Dog-day cicadas droned through August. We let the little green inchworms walk around on our hands. The red and brown wooly bears curled up in a tight ball as soon as we touched them. Cute. They ate grass, but we thought they were a defoliating tree pest, associating them with the wispy tents strung across branches in late summer. But those tents belonged to the fall webworms. Sometimes we took a long stick and poked at their tents, trying to stir up them up. Ladybugs were always welcome.

We climbed trees—the higher the better—but only hardwood trees. Firs had too many limbs; pines got pitch on your hands, whose removal required kerosene or gasoline. Some kids nearer to town made a clubhouse out of old boards and, for a roof, two rusty sheets of corrugated steel. Inside it was dark and damp. We ate white bread and onions and sour green apples with salt on them. We played kick-the-can down at Foster's, putting the can in the middle of the road to make it more dangerous to get to. Accusations of cheating or poor sportsmanship led to manure fights. Why did our parents let us back in the house?

In the fields we caught toads and got warts—what did we care? Frogs were larger but slipperier, and they had the inconvenient habit of jumping back in the brook. Out back towards the woods there was a shallow well lined with stones that housed a perennial spring. It never went dry, even if there was no other well with water for miles. On my approach, big bullfrogs leapt for safety. I would lie down on the rocks and put my face in the cold water; on the other side pairs of eyes floated just above the surface like small, unblinking Brussels sprouts.

Nothing was finer to stave off boredom on a summer afternoon than a war in the woods with BB guns. The preferred model had a lever action, like a Winchester Model 94. When asked where you are going, be prepared with some breezy lie like, "I'm going to help Bobbie wash his father's car" (his father took the car to Lewiston this morning), or, "I'm going to help Bobbie dig worms for his fishing trip" (not only

Church Hill Road in Summer.

does Bobbie hate fishing, they don't have a septic tank, so you can't get the best worms). Notice that the best lies always have some aspect of usefulness about them. Pure goofing off can sometimes make the voice less assured.

Stalking the enemy brings out the age-old atavism of the hunter, genetically reinforced over the millennia to aid survival. You practice moving stealthily, without breaking branches, putting your foot down slowly to reduce the crunching of the leaves. You stop and peer down low so you can see feet belonging to a body hidden by evergreens. Or you get in a depression in the ground and wait for the enemy to come to you. There he is—fifty feet away, and *Pow!* A surprised "Ouch!" tells you all you need to know. No shooting above the armpits. Although technically free to roam anywhere in the maybe three thousand acres on the east side of Church Hill Road, hunting for hours without finding anybody, friend or foe, kind of reduced the fun.

When I was ten, I went to Winslow Fair for a day with a friend. His mother dropped us off and, I guess, picked us up in the afternoon. I had money, the twenty-five dollars I had saved up from haying—on our own, no supervision, and in a place where I could pretend to be having real fun. Not quite Carnegie Hall, but I would settle. I bought the usual things: food, rides. Then I saw a camera I just had to have— fourteen dollars—and with limitless naiveté fell for the spiel of the hawker. Probably worth all of fifty cents. When I got home, my mother was appalled; she was counting on my twenty-five dollars to pay for an extension course that she needed to maintain her teaching certificate. I overpaid for the camera and spent my otherwise-needed money attempting to have what would be publicly considered a good time. I felt really bad. We drove over to the fair, and she returned the camera. I'm not sure what happened to the money.

Chapter XIII

Church and the DAR

We went to church for a few months, the Baptist church at the top of the rise past Gilleys. The name of the road has nothing to do with the church but rather with the Churches, who lived there in the nineteenth century. The minister's name was, somewhat unfortunately, Weavil or more formally, the Reverend E. (Claude) R. Weavil. He came by the haying operation several times, trying to fan the flames of religious enthusiasm. He was always well received but found little enthusiasm and less commitment. An unwilling farmer could always blame those pesky, time-sensitive chores like milking, mowing and cultivating, meaning, if the sun is shinin' we fer shur ain't comin' 'cause we gotta git in the hay. He was understanding: like Bildad, he believed that Sabbath or no, one should not reject Heaven's gifts, among which surely was a sunny day.

They found out my mother played the piano and promptly drafted her for the organist. She was a world-class sight-reader. At rehearsals they were amazed. Having suffered from hip trouble since her late twenties, she did have some problem swinging her feet back and forth on the pedal board.

On Sunday morning, I put on my best clothes, and off we went to church, the three of us, my father dismissing it as "so much malarkey." I didn't know what to make of it all, the minister's enthusiasm, the hymnal with its onionskin paper and flexible covers, a bit worn looking but serviceable and with an endless supply of right-sounding songs. Services were generally decorous—not like the previous congregation of Holy Rollers. My friend Allen used to peek in the window and see the likes of George French lying on his back kicking up his feet in religious fervor. Then again, E. R. freely consigned Catholics to perdition's flames for abandoning the true Church. Where did that put me? I was in neither camp. What was I supposed to feel? I was sensitive enough to know that if asked, offering my father's views on religion was the wrong thing to do.

Church was rather thinly attended: fully one-third of the congregation came with the reverend in his large van fitted out with extra seats. I recognized a few neighbors. On the outside, the building was used-to-be-grey clapboards, the inside rather open and unfinished: a dusty floor, pews in two sections extending to the back, and a raised area for the choir and pulpit. The high points of the service were my mother playing, putting some change in the collection plate, and attending a sort of Sunday school run in a room off to the side. There they gave us pages of religious themes to color, and had a nifty felt board on which you could stick figures and animals to illustrate a story. I thought that was particularly ingenious.

The faithful were called to services by a sound system in the church belfry. The speakers, a bit overwhelmed by the demand for volume, produced scratchy, unintelligible hymns. This scrannel, electronic carillon lacked the uninhibited, rolling exuberance of real bells. Outclassed as it was by many home door chimes, it failed to produce religious fervor in even the already committed.

When my mother got sick, all this stopped. We never looked back. I think for her church attendance was in the same category as joining the local chapter of the DAR—a way to meet people and gain social access to neighbors, particularly after the previous years of near-total isolation. The Daughters of the American Revolution came and went fairly quickly. She never spoke of it, but as the wife of a New York Jew, ex-communist duck farmer, she might have gotten less than a warm welcome. Yes, they did have an outreach program, but it didn't reach that far. And anyway, they were all related to captains and field-grade officers, while she was only related to a private. It was their loss.

Chapter XIV

Learning Latin

My brother was very smart. Jeremy sat in the back of the classroom and read novels inside his plane-geometry book. To provide some real intellectual challenge, my father, when Jeb got out of the seventh grade, began tutoring him in Latin. He did great. He started second year Latin as a high school freshman. Then I got out of the seventh grade, and my father decided I should learn Latin, too. That was a mistake. I was riven by emotional turmoil, a poor studier and an even poorer memorizer, and was for sure not interested in competing head-on with my brother, who had been walking on water for some years already. Why couldn't he have taught me Greek?

When he was young, my father failed to get what he needed, so children always remained an abstraction for him. It is a terrible but common sentence in this world: to be defined by what was neglected. He meant well, but was unable to talk to a child or figure out what they might need. He held a baby stiffly, his arms extended, as one would hold a raccoon dead since last week.

I muddled along. Translations were agony. My father knew where the story was going by the third word; I hadn't figured it out by the last. Then there were all those pesky cases and genders for the nouns, with which the definite article and adjective had to agree. There were so many possible choices a guy couldn't even guess! The verbs must have spent the entire Second Punic War conjugating and otherwise asexually reproducing, since there were so many forms. By the end of the lesson, I couldn't tell an ablative absolute from a gerund.

"What in Christ is an ablative absolute?"

"When I look it up, there's always too much verbiage that I have no interest in struggling through. It's something like the first clause in the sentence, 'With Caesar dead, Brutus was free to make lunch.' The ablative is the case, and the absolute means 1) there is only one ablative allowed in the sentence, and 2) the clause has no substantive connection to the rest of the sentence. But you should really look it up."

"Okay, sometime in this life . . . And a gerund?"

"A noun-like word substituted for a verb phrase or clause: 'Swinging, the kid hit the ball over the fence.'

"Fascinating—"

"Spare me the sarcasm, thank you."

He saved his loudest groans for when I—

God, how could I have got this wrong?—

confused the ablative or instrumental "with" (Gaius ground the wheat *with* a millstone) and the accompaniment "with" (Gaius went to town *with* his friend). I constructed riotous sentences: Gaius ground the grain while walking along with the millstone; Gaius went to town riding on his friend. He never laughed. It was torture. Vocatives stealthily tied my shoelaces together, ablatives of attendant circumstances leered at me from behind the toaster, passive periphrastics held my coat and snickered. At some point he allowed as how, since he had taught all this stuff to my brother, I should already know it.

"So you couldn't do Latin and you didn't like music. Didn't they try to teach you other stuff—they knew so much."

"I got a great deal from them: values, ethics, knowledge. But at this distance it doesn't seem as if it was actually taught, but rather that I absorbed it. Whenever I know something without knowing it, it comes from my parents. And though my father didn't actually teach me what he knew, I got even by learning it anyway."

"What particularly do you mean?"

"For instance, the power of language. I can read something and know that it is great with knowing little more than the words themselves."

"How did this express itself?"

"For instance, I'm reading a book of modern poetry and prose— years ago. The piece was called "Watchman, What of the Night?" I knew that that phrase was special in some powerful way, but nothing more about it. Some years later I found the source. It's Isaiah!

"Then New York had a program called Poetry Underground: they scattered posters with poems (or parts of them) among the many ads in each subway car. In this case they only had room to print the last five lines."

>   I have seen nothing of rivers, mountains or the sea
>   But the light of Buenos Aires made itself my friend
>   And I forge the verses of my life and my death with the light of the street
>   Great, long-suffering street
>   You are the only music my soul has understood.*

"I immediately said to myself, 'That is a great poem.'

"Ten years or so later, I'm wandering in a big bookstore near Columbia University—I think it was called Labyrinth at the time. Find books by Borges. Find a book of his poetry—in Spanish. All I remembered of the poem at this point was that the translated title on the subway poster was "Street With a Pink Corner Store." I no longer remembered the text. Flipping through the book, I found it! Calle con almacén rosado. And sure enough, it is a homerun: in English it is a homerun; in Spanish it is simply remarkable. I get this ability to spot stuff from my father, and it was a great gift."

---

*Selected Poems: Jorge Luis Borges. Viking, Alexander Coleman, ed., translation by Stephen Kessler © 1999.

Chapter XV

Water

Water was a problem. The brook, having no real source except runoff and rain, shrank to a turbid trickle by the middle of the summer. Our dug well, all fifteen feet of it, fared little better: the well digger must have certified it during a heavy rainstorm. It was an anxiety, dependably inadequate. However, drilling an artesian well cost seven dollars a foot: if you were lucky you got water at thirty-five feet; if not, you might have to go a hundred and fifty feet—too great a financial risk. A water shortage is serious on a farm. Our birds needed a lot of water to grow, and the family needed some water to continue to live normally. The first casualty was taking a bath. Once in a while a cloudburst put enough water through the short downspout at the corner of the house to make a cold but effective shower, but time and space made this a one-man solution. No vibrating head on this shower, no massaging needle spray! Rather like standing under a very tall faucet with a large bore and low pressure. And you had to be quick—quick to strip off your clothes and quick to rinse. No telling when the rain would stop, leaving you soaped up and stranded. We usually fell back on Togus Pond, a nondescript body of water about seven miles from the house. In a state with hundreds of similar small lakes, Togus had nothing to recommend it but proximity and a certain raw accessibility. In New Jersey it would be classified as a lake, with lots of rules and a self-promoting homeowners association; in Maine, it was an accident.

The state, years before, had built up the low causeway which crossed a narrow arm of the pond, using gravel and boulders (and possibly rocks from our garden); then they put a road on the causeway, paved it, and gave it official status as State Route 105. Locals referred to it as South Belfast Avenue, to distinguish it from Route 3, North Belfast Avenue. Since the causeway sloped down into the water, the shore was a legal no-man's-land. Here we would arrive on a summer afternoon, soap and towel in hand, and inch our way into the murky coldness. It was always cold, but cold is relative, and the need to have some fun swimming around was great; the bath at the end was convenient if not essential. The beach was a mother's nightmare: no wading here—three steps and you were in seven feet of water. After a short period of messing around and exhibiting an uncalled-for level of bravado and enjoyment, we sat on a rock and soaped up what was exposed and then jumped in the water and soaped up what was not. A rinse followed. The towels were too few and too thin to get really dry. Home we went, ears gurgling.

A somewhat more delicate area that a water shortage affected was the bathroom. Now as long as we had the privy, a water shortage produced less of a problem. No moving parts, no flushing required. When we got one of those fancy porcelain jobs with the handle and this fascinating ball float in the tank and a noise like Charybdis on a good day, having running water assumed an added urgency. Backs to the wall, we resorted to manual flushes: lugging pails of water from the now much-shrunk brook or saving the water from washing the clothes. We were way ahead on the recycling curve!

But enough of hardship! After a swim and a bath or, for the older set, a bath and a swim, nothing could be finer than a cookout. Our barbecue appeared to be a pile of random auto parts temporarily stacked together in a chop shop. The frame was from a washing machine planted upside down, with all the parts stripped off. In the middle, an upturned garbage-can lid—or possibly the bottom four inches of the tub of the aforementioned washing machine neatly cut off with an acetylene torch—held the wood or charcoal. On edge, just inside the tub's rim, was a long, wide arc of metal that could be swung to the most advantageous position to block the wind. Above, some ill-fitting grates rested on the frame. Rust and neglect sat heavily on this contraption.

But balled-up newspaper, some thin sticks of kindling, several bolts of dry hardwood and a knowing hand would produce, in about thirty minutes, a bed of glowing coals giving an intense dry heat. Franks and burgers, steaks (if some woeful-looking cut was on sale), corn that had been on a living plant less than two hours before—hey, who cares if the toilet doesn't work! Having non-functioning plumbing was a great way to keep company away or, more importantly, relatives from New York, who might take the lack of amenities less in the spirit of pioneer virtue and more as an intolerable inconvenience, country living or no.

Chapter XVI

The Florida Connection

For a number of years, my grandmother sent money to my mother so she could fly down to Florida in the summer for a visit. We took her to the Augusta State Airport, and off she went on a venerable DC-3—you know, one of those tipped-up, stubby planes with two props, where you had to pull yourself up the center aisle by grabbing the seat backs. DC-3s had been flying since the 30s. I think Northeast Airlines acquired their fleet at government auction after WWII. The dusty cabins, the narrow seats, the buzzing, the poor insulation—every seat was near a different hydraulic pump that whined at unsettling moments in the flight. These absences were very tough on my father, producing a variety of somatic symptoms of stress, some internal, some external. If we had had money, we could have gone out to the Roseland Diner once in a while, but as we did not, he fell to cooking with a resigned lack of enthusiasm. Breakfast and lunch were whatever was around. His favorite dinners were either giant garden salads with cottage cheese and sour cream on the side, producing no pots to wash, or noodles with fried onions, this time with the cottage cheese mixed in. I thought he was a great cook.

In June of the year that Jeb got out of the eighth grade, he was invited to come to Florida, also. He came back with money to buy a Raleigh three-speed English bike—that's what we called bikes with the narrow tires. After my eighth-grade graduation, I went with a friend and his mother to Reid State Park, a large park on one of the many points which jut out into the Gulf of Maine. It faces southeast, in which direction the next landfall might be the Azores, three thousand miles away. We screamed running in and out of the fifty-degree breakers, then had an all-you-can-eat hotdog roast. I had asked, but was told that Florida wasn't for me. I suppose some evil intersection of smell, noisy enthusiasm, and impetuousness doomed my chances for the big trip. I wasn't quick enough to say, "Well, I'll settle for New York." Anyway, by this time my haying skills were worth three dollars an afternoon. I continued to ride the girls' bike my parents had bought secondhand for five dollars some years before.

Chapter XVII

The New Room

On some summer evenings, the upstairs being too hot for sleeping, I took advantage of the privilege of sleeping in the "new room." The new room was just that, a room in the back of the house we built in what was an unfinished, pit-like space with a dirt floor. There they had once stored wood for the kitchen stove or maybe coal for the furnace: it was a dark, scary place. The room had fresh, plasterboard walls and hardwood flooring. It had a door to the outside: we never used it, because the first step was a three-foot drop to the back yard. Here also was the second of the two new appliances I remember: a large, upright Amana freezer, most of which was taken up by poultry that didn't sell. The old and the damaged and the unsalable had their own shelf—those were the ones we ate. Vegetables from our garden that my mother carefully "put by" filled any remaining space—I'm sure she enjoyed being freed from the drudgeries of canning.

I slept on what was originally the bottom of a high-riser, right underneath an open window. Through it came a chorus of whip-poor-wills, uncountable peepers and crickets, and the staccato-tremolo who-who-ing of a screech owl, the whole punctuated by the thick, nasal baritone of the bullfrogs and overpowered occasionally by a raucous outburst from the ducks and geese, probably settling some territorial issue. From somewhere far, a thrush sang its final song of the evening. The night air, cool, moist, insistent, burdened by memory and laden with immense distance, and bearing the smells of the surrounding fields and trees, tumbled in on my chest.

Chapter XVIII

Haying

[Off Haying, August 1955]

The summer after I got out of the fourth grade, my brother and I started working for the farmer next door.

"So how old does that make you?"

"Let's see. I was nine and three quarters and Jeb was eleven and a half."

Born in 1886, Ernest Cunningham was "old" when we first knew him: small, tough, wiry, with thin hair plastered back, unusually big hands, and a plain, honest face. Not much over five feet and weighing maybe 150 pounds, he moved deliberately and worked with a restrained efficiency. He had worked in the woods with veterans of the Civil War, yet younger and stronger men could still not work shoulder to shoulder with him for a day. He was from the old school and used horses to bring in the hay; we helped a little and were paid a dollar for an afternoon's work. As we grew, we could help more, so every year our salary went up fifty cents. We were rich, and as this employment lasted the best part of the summer, our parents weren't burdened by having to provide any diversions or interesting outings.

"You couldn't have hayed every day. What happened if it rained? Did you go to friends'?"

"Rainy days might be spent going to friends—well, as long as they were approved friends, bickering incessantly over a card game, sorting buttons, or rereading the first three sentences of À la recherche du temps perdu. This latter title was part of our small library, its cover indelibly imprinted in my memory."

Forty years later I was at a friend's house, when, across the room, I saw on the spine of a book high up on a shelf its unmistakable arrangement of tan, brown, and blue.

Remembrance of Things Past, while a little longwinded, was definitely on the approved list. One couldn't be too careful in this area—my father once laughed at me for reading *The Grapes of Wrath* immediately after finishing *Ivanhoe*. I couldn't even keep my genres straight! On rainy days we couldn't hay, of course, because wet hay in a barn causes disastrous fires due to spontaneous combustion.

"I told you about the fires I saw, didn't I?"

"Just the one down the road at Stone's."

"There was that one—I guess we were haying and heard about it. There, because of its proximity, the fire jumped to the farmhouse. What a loss. And there were two others when I was already working or going to school. Flames fifty feet in the air. You can't get anywhere near a fire like that without protective equipment. Scary."

The nutritional value of grass starts to decline immediate it hits the ground behind the mower, so a farmer who needs good hay to feed out over the winter is always under some pressure to gather it up. But what to do when caught by an unexpected thunder shower, or the hay is very stout? Tedder it. A horse-drawn tedder is a two-wheeled affair having behind the driver an open mechanism from the back of which a number of steel arms extend. Projecting from the end of each arm were long fingers of heavy, spring-loaded wire. Via several clever gears, the horizontal mechanism moved counter to the forward motion of the tedder, and the tines on the reciprocating arms fluffed up the damp hay like a cruel body-enhancer brush in a hair salon.

Haying had an important side benefit: it kept back the bushes, ever eager to reclaim a field that some nineteenth-century farmer struggled for years to clear using chains and a team of oxen to pull out stumps, often building stone walls with the endless rocks. The mower, a solid steel affair with metal lugged wheels, was drawn by a team. On one side of the adjustable support for the seat was proudly written in donut-fat, raised letters: "John Deere 1901." With one hand Ernest held four reins, one between each finger, and turned the horses by holding fast on two and letting the other two slide. With the other hand he raised and lowered the six-foot-long cutter bar, whose large teeth and shiny, reciprocating blade, driven by a gear train from the motion of the mower, justly inspired fear. The lever controlling the bar was awkwardly placed, requiring the operator to push down behind his shoulder, and as the bar had to go from horizontal to vertical with a small throw of this lever, the mechanical advantage favored the cutter bar. To raise it was no small feat, particularly for a man of sixty-five, particularly while controlling a team of horses. In all the years I hayed, I was never able to do it.

The hay lay as it fell for a day, maybe two, if it wasn't hot and dry. At about one o'clock he called down to us, "Okay, boys!" and we headed up to his barn wearing our straw hats, looking like a couple of country hayseeds. Grab a pitchfork from the barn, slide the tines around a vertical brace on the hayrack, climb onto it—either by stepping up and over from a wheel hub, climbing the ladder at the back, or hoisting yourself through one of the cutouts in the bottom that gave the wheels sufficient clearance to allow the rack to turn sharply—and off we bounced to that afternoon's field. The closest were the thirty-five-or-so acres behind Ernest's barn. The others lay across the road and further down Blair Road, a patchwork of irregular shapes, whose sole benefit to mankind was to produce a thin crop of hay year after year, and even this was only valuable to a farmer who did not have modern machinery. A man with a tractor and a hay baler wanted large, level, stout hay fields.

Woods surrounded the fields on which we worked, or if there was an adjacent field, it was set off by a line of small trees and brush and the inevitable stone wall. The roll of the fields was just as it was when they were first cleared, the contours only of interest to the extent that they might influence how we got the hay. After we drove off with it, the field, with its short, sharp stubble, became like a thing discarded long ago, whose one-time importance is tiresome now even to think of.

I felt bad for the woods because nobody treasured them, or found them worth exploring. I tried, but I was never allowed to know what I was looking for. The woods remain unsatisfied, the fields now only visible in memory.

Riding in an empty hayrack required certain sailor-like skills in order not to be pitched about (or off) when we went over the inevitable bumps, ruts, groundhog holes, and ledge outcroppings, or the horse, feeling pressure on the breeching straps—

croup strap

"On the what?"

"On the breeching—that part of the harness that prevents a wagon from running up onto the horse, like when you have to go down a hill or try to back up. It's pronounced 'britching,' not the way it is written."

"What'a they look like?"

"Heavy leather straps are attached to that part of a work harness which goes around the back of a horse's thighs; they then attach to hooks built onto the shafts—"

"And the shafts are—"

"The two long pole-like pieces of wood projecting from the frame of the wagon or whatever is being pulled. As you back the horse between the shafts you have to raise them so they get inserted into their carrier loops on the girth. Anyway, as I said, the breeching keeps the wagon from running up on the horse in a downgrade. But a horse generally does not like any pressure from the breeching and so often breaks into a trot to keep ahead of this annoyance."

"And what are those shiny things with the knobs that stick up over the horse's back?"

"They are the tops of the hames. First you put on the collar, so the load will be pulled by the horse's shoulders and not by his neck. Came into use in Europe around the twelfth century because, in dragging the big blocks of stone needed to build their cathedrals, they were choking their draft animals. Anyway, the collar has a groove in it toward the front, and into this groove are rigged the hames, which have the shiny knobs on them. The heavy leather straps, called the tugs, go from the hames to the whippletree, and thus the power of the horse is transferred to the wagon."

"And you know all this stuff why?"

"Forget it. You wouldn't understand—"

So from feeling the pressure from the breeching, the horse might make a little run on a downgrade. The added velocity had serious implications. Sitting on the hard floorboards was uncomfortable. One could stand and hold on to the ladder-like back of the rack, but who wanted to stand? The most grownup way was to sit slightly sideways on one of the heavy rails forming the top of the rack's sides and keep one foot looped securely behind an upright, rolling your upper body back and forth in response to the pitching wagon. The other regular helper during haying, an older man from the neighborhood named Fred Stevens, would unloose a torrent of abuse on the pitching wagon, but saved his most savage words for the ledge outcroppings. Most of what he said will not be printed, but in keeping with the times, the printable part of his fervent wish was that "one of those goddamned atomic bombs would come and blow every last goddamned rock out of this field!"

Unless the raking was done in the fore-noon, Fred drove the hay rake to that day's field. Pulled by one horse, this large-wheeled rig had a basket-like affair along the back with curved, independently mounted tines that dragged along the ground, collecting the hay. When the basket was full, it was, without stopping the horse, "dumped" by pushing forward on a lever; this in turn raised the tines in unison and left behind whatever hay had been collected. The lever was then smoothly returned to its down position, and a new collection started. This was repeated again and again, back and forth, until the field had long, parallel windrows wandering across it, part of the art of raking being the ability to dump the rake at exactly the same point on each pass. The stouter the hay, the closer the windrows.

My brother, being older, built the load, while I bunched. Just pitch the hay into the wagon and drive to the barn? Not at all. It was an art, a sweaty, dusty art. Consider the fact that the top rail of the rack was six feet from the ground, yet the rack was filled to twice that height before heading home. The last pitchfork loads were delivered with one hand, the man on the ground standing on tiptoe, the one on top reaching down with his fork to grab it. And consider also that this now-unsupported load had to survive the lurching trip back to the barn. The initial loads from each bunch were delivered from the ground intact. These were always moved to the outside edges of the load and rocked into place to bind them. The smaller, cleanup forkfuls went in the middle. When the load was low, there was not much to do but tread down the load to build a solid base and to weave a "floor" over the wide wheel openings. By the time it became necessary, a grown man could stand over these openings with confidence.

Treading down the load was just that—walking over the puffy hay to drive the air out of it and, particularly at the edges, to make it knit tightly with the hay around it. Once the hay reached the height of the rails, the load was built out so that it overhung them on each side. This required careful positioning by the person on top and circumspect treading down, since the edges were now well beyond the point of solid support.

I generally bunched, that is, I made an opening in the windrow for the wagon. I built mounds of ready-to-be-pitched-in hay on both sides of this opening. As I worked ahead of the operation, I was usually alone. Here again, the job was a bit more than it might seem. The opening needed to be so positioned that an equal amount of hay, over time, was pitched on from both sides. The rake had already accomplished a certain amount of alignment and compression, and the buncher needed to take advantage of it, as bunching was building small hay stacks in layers, rather than pitching the hay together in a frothy pile. I had to cull out the swail, the wide, rough-leafed grasses growing near water or wet areas. More formally called sweet flag, by reputation, anyway, it stopped cows from producing milk. Stout hay made big hay stacks—"he-bunches" they called them. A good bunch allowed those pitching on to pick up one edge with the fork, pin it over into the middle and fully insert the tines; then, placing the palm on the end of the handle and the back of that hand high up against the inside of the thigh, they levered the entire pile into the air in one motion and placed it neatly on the rack. What was left was scraped up in a minute, and so on to the next windrow.

Occasionally the mower uncovered a sparrow's nest on the ground in an out-of-the-way thicket. Once the cover was gone, the mother bird never came back. The eggs, four or five, were barely half an inch long, with soft, brown, speckles and shells as flexible as the skin on boiled milk.

Finding a nest was a thrill, a disclosure of something normally hidden. But, in that we had driven the mother away and the eggs would never hatch, such a find also carried with it a sense of loss, of abandonment. I felt a dim responsibility but was unable to act on it. I regret that I never did—I veered away and walked on.

Voles also built their nests in the grass. Sometimes the depression occupied by the nest was low enough to escape the hay rake. The babies were the size of small, unshelled peanuts, pink and hairless. These I also investigated, then moved on; grownups angrily stomped on them—they ate the grain.

Moving from windrow to windrow, the load rose. When no more could be thrown on, it was off to the barn, the hayrack a moving mow worthy of Breughel, the big draft horse Tommy, with legs like tree trunks and hooves the size of dinner plates, straining at the traces. Crows took possession of the field as soon as we left. When we were working across the road—

"Where is 'across the road'?"

"The other side of the road from the barn—let's see—that would be the west side."

"And why did this make a difference?"

"Because the wagon always came up Blair Road and had to ascend a small but significant hill before gaining the paved road and the driveway to the barn. Everyone but the driver was told to get off, saving weight. The driver could only see traffic coming in one direction—from down the hill—yet had to commit fully to making the hill, since it was approached at a bit of a run, and even Tommy could not restart a big load once it stopped on such an incline."

"So let me understand this: a fully loaded wagon, pulled by a single horse, moving at a slow trot, pulls onto a paved road without the operator being able to see traffic? Just like that? Sounds like a disaster waiting to happen. You must have had road guards—"

"Road guards? What are road guards?"

"You should remember them from the Army. The two guys just behind the forward corners of the marching formation ran into the road and stood in the middle of it to warn approaching vehicles and stayed there until everyone was safely across."

Henry and Ernest

"Oh, yeah. But our road was so infrequently traveled that pulling a loaded hay rack into the road never resulted in disaster."

Additionally, Blair Road had not been graded in decades and the road's cross-section where it met the pavement was even steeper than Church Hill Road. The effect of this slope was magnified because the driver had already started to turn the horse up the hill—away from possible oncoming traffic—so the final lurch of the wagon, as it made the turn, was a real heart-stopper.

Into the barn went the wagon, while we went into the cowshed for a cold drink out of the hose. Jerry, Ernest's second horse, was smaller. If the raking was finished, the whole rig might come back; otherwise I unhooked the horse from the rake and led it back by the halter, since it was essential for unloading. Leading the horse this way made me feel particularly useful and grown up. The older and stronger workers went into the mow, which, as the summer progressed, rose higher and higher on each side of the central area now occupied by the wagon. In the end, the mow could only be accessed by one of the tall ladders nailed vertically to a big beam. Mow work was hot and dusty; when near the roof and the hay needed pushing under the eves, it was wretched. Wretched also was treading the big piles of loose hay that came whooshing down off the fork—stepping in a soft spot put you right to your armpits in the stuff. You sweated in a swirling haze of pollen, chaff and dust while barn swallows buzzed you for getting near their nests. When I got older, I got promoted from the mow to walking the "leading-out" horse.

"Why did you need the second horse?"

"You have to imagine that the level of the hay was ten feet or more above the top of the hay in the rack. So how did the new hay actually get up there?"

"I figured you just pitched it up the way you pitched it on."

"Impossible. We used a hay fork. Imagine a large, U-shaped two-pronged fork with a lever at the top of each prong. These levers, when pulled up, caused points housed in the tips of the prongs to rotate inward ninety degrees, locking them at right angles. These levers were attached to a light rope called the "snatch line." The larger rope for the fork itself was reeved through a number of wooden blocks or large pulleys—the first one being up near the roof on the active side of the barn—and thence, via an improbably complicated path, out the barn door itself. To that end was attached the leading-out horse. The man on the load muscled the fork down into the hay, set the bottom points by pulling up the levers, hollered 'Okay!' and stepped circumspectly out of the way. I led the horse directly away from the barn, which as you might expect raised the enormous load of hay up to the mow. When the load was in position, another cry 'Whoa!' told me to stop. The man on the rack jerked on the small rope, the points rotated back into the fork proper, and the load came swishing down to be put away by those in the mow. I turned the horse around and walked it back, while the man on the load, feeling the main rope go slack, pulled the fork back by the snatch line for another load. At the barn, I again turned the horse around for another run, being careful not to step over the rope."

"Why couldn't you just loop around?"

"Caused kinks, which might cause the rope to break."

It broke occasionally for other reasons, causing no end of cussing and effort to get it back on the blocks after being spliced—and put those in the mow in danger of fielding a load which would include the heavy metal fork. Those working stood respectfully out of the way as the loads came up.

The odds and ends of hay were pitched out onto the barn floor. In quick succession: unhitch Jerry and put him in his stall, unless we needed him back at the operation; grab a donut or a cookie if one was offered; grab another drink at the barrel; back the rack out of the barn and turn it around; grab your fork, and hop on the rack for another load.

After the second load, "the Missus" offered a "lunch" for all the workers, said lunch consisting of homemade lemonade, a sandwich, often with some sort of meat, and a piece of cake. Only if you are dead would you have trouble figuring out how good that food tasted! We sat around the kitchen table, whose plastic tablecloth smelled of suet and whose folds were worn from countless scrubbings so that when spread it seemed to have tan lines of latitude. The loud ticking of their cuckoo clock filled the gaps in what little conversation there was. Pearl served the food with palsied hands. The lemons floated hazily in the pitcher, its outside sweating in the humidity. A grinding whir and a tiny door. A blur of yellow catapulted out from the clock's innards. The appropriate number of cuckoos having been sounded, the captive bird was swallowed bodily. The clock, satisfied, returned to its ticking.

Then back for the last load of the afternoon, or as Ernest would say, "another lud." Home we went, sweat having glued hayseeds and dirt to our immature bodies, happily clutching our hard-earned money. Walking out of Ernest's driveway, life was grand; walking into our driveway, the sky was never quite so blue.

Chapter XIX

Summer Chores

Around Memorial Day we planted a garden in the small field that faced the front of the house. Unfortunately, it opened to the north, thereby failing to get the most from Maine's stingy growing season, and for this reason my mother started certain vegetables inside or in a cold frame. We bought the tomato plants from the hardware store. The soil was heavy and clayey, making drainage poor—so poor in fact that the plowing and harrowing had to wait for a spell of dry weather, else the tractor might get stuck in the mud. What that field needed was a couple of truckloads of sand. The garden was slow to start (cold soil), slow to grow (not enough sun), and soonest to suffer from frost (we were at the lowest point on the road). In the fall we bought a load or two of cow manure from Ernest—a dollar a load. Two loads were two dollars plus a drink, but only by negotiation, else, since we were a neighbor, his price for two loads would also have been one dollar!

He stopped by one day when he saw we were finished with the slaughter operation. Mommy had her schoolwork spread out on the kitchen table.

"Hiya, Missus. Hiya, boys. Hi, Henry. How many luds you want this yeah?"

"Oh, I guess we'll take two," my father replied.

"Next weekend, I guess. Seth said he'd come over."

"That sounds fine." Daddy fished out two dollars. "How about a drink, Ernest?"

"Sounds good, Henry. Thanks."

He once asked my father if wanting a drink after a day's work put him on the slippery path to being an alcoholic.

"How's Pearl?"

"Oh, pretty good, pretty good. She gets around. She suffers in the winter." His voice shook a little, and he looked away briefly.

"Yeah, I'll bet. The boys said you talked about getting a new roof on the barn before long."

"Yeah, have to. But I ain't doin' it myself. I'm too old, Henry, just too old. Goin' to hire it done. Expensive. At times I think I should just close up and find a rent in town, what with the wood and the cows and the ha'ne. Doctor's awful dear. See ads for big places in Augusta for $125 a month, furnished and het."

"Well, no one would blame you. You've worked a long time."

"Yeah, that's right, that's right. Started workin' fulltime when I was fourteen—in 1900—haulin' coal with four horses." My father shook his head. "Got a letter from your father." Ernest continued. "He wants me to talk to Fred Stevens about repaying the loan."

My father groaned. "A loan? Pop loaned him money?"

"Oh, yeah," Ernest continued. "He always carries a bundle around with him. Takes it out and offers to loan me or Fred money. I was so hard up with the doctor's bills I did borrow twenty dollars from him in the summer, but I paid it back. Fred borrowed a hundred. If I have to, I'll pay it myself." Dismay showed on Mommy's face. "What's he do that for?" he continued. "He ought'a have a guard'een, at his age he needs a guard'een."

"He certainly does," my father agreed, chagrined. "And more—"

"He does it to obligate you, so he can call on you for help," Mommy offered. "I'm sorry Fred fell into his trap."

Garden, Augusta, 1953

"He's okay, he's okay," Ernest retreated, worried that he had overstepped the family's sensibilities. "He gave me a nice cut, a real nice cut, said he brought it all the way from New York." He changed the subject.

"That dog of yourn okay? The boys said he was tore up pretty bad."

"He was. Some other dog, I suppose a dog, just about killed him. Vet had to put him to sleep to operate. Expensive."

"I'll bet. Mollison's after me to let him dig a ditch across my fields and lay pipe, so's he can get water from that spring out there. I may need that water someday. He's always drivin' the latest crumb-plated auto-mobile, ain't he? Why can't he drill a well?"

"I don't know," my father answered sympathetically. "Doesn't he already have a drilled well?"

"He does, but doesn't give enough water. But, I need the money. He tol' me yistahday he's got some outa-town folks comin', n'they want to hunt pahtridge out back. I told him okay. I don't know if thea's any out thea," he added, smiling. "More likely pheasants." He started to collect himself. "Well, betta go—caows are waitin', always waitin'. Thanks for the drink, Henry. See you, boys."

Daddy saw him out and walked with him to the road. "Why'd he go with him?" I asked my mother.

"Probably to discuss the money and his father," she said.

After the garden was in, the whole family went out to work on it once a week. Some weeded, some hoed, some thinned. Weeding was fussy work, done kneeling. Hoeing broke up the soil around the plants, kept the roots covered, and gave the stalks some extra strength by heaping soil around them. Seeds were always planted too thickly, so we selectively uprooted some, always trying to leave the best. Root crops like carrots had to be thinned to give some of them room to grow. In a row of corn, the runts went first. We used to thin the radishes by pulling one out of the ground and eating it, first making a halfhearted attempt to get off the dirt. They tasted better before they were washed. On tomato plants, branches growing out of the 'V' made by the main stem and an existing branch were just foliage; we broke off these suckers, forcing the plant to work on the fruit. Working on tomato plants leaves your hands slick and musky and slightly green.

The rocks were in endless supply, small ones pushed to the surface by the heaving of the frozen ground each winter, football-sized ones and larger lurking just out of sight. We made some effort to get rid of them, but it was stoop work and therefore unpopular. If nothing else needed weeding, hoeing or thinning, or possibly my parents felt the remaining garden jobs were too delicate for me, yet it was still too early to go goof off somewhere or maybe read the Sears catalog—

"You read the Sears Catalog, too? Which sections did you like?"

"I liked the tools and the machinery, with which I could fix up the house and make all manner of woodworking projects and landscaping improvements."

"Clothes?"

"Not so much. They were still using headless models, then attempting to make them more lifelike by randomly pasting on heads, sometimes at an angle that suggested its owner might have been in a bad accident. And with the sports stuff, of course, I would be the star of the Little League team. And I always spent time trying to imagine what was under the ladies' underwear."

"I know, girdles were big back then."

"I couldn't figure out what exactly was their function . . ."

Picking up rocks was the job of choice and could productively fill any amount of time. Dragging a pail which got ever heavier, you backed up between rows until the pail was as full as your strength allowed. Staggering under the load, you emptied the pail in the no-man's-land between the garden proper and Ernest's overgrown stone wall. Hoeing or weeding, a pail for rocks was your constant companion, though it was a losing proposition—to make real progress we would need to dig up the whole garden with an excavator but would have happily settled for a platoon of rock pickers.

We used Rotenone to combat leaf-eating bugs. However, if something was nibbling the leaves of the tomato plants, it was time to look for tomato worms. They hatched from the eggs of the hawk moth—we would sometimes find one on the porch in the morning, capable only of buzzing uselessly in circles on the floor. Their compact, cartridge-shaped bodies exhibited a kind of fierce coarseness. Though well camouflaged, the worms were still easy to spot, since they might be as big as your little finger. We pulled them off by grabbing the horn on their head with pliers; they writhed and emitted clicking noises in protest. You could have used your hand, but our phylogenetic distaste for all things crawly dictated a tool. No tool? Screw up your courage, and in one motion yank it off, drop it on the ground and stomp on it.

We had a pretty standard garden, a bit heavy on the squash and green beans, since these were stored or canned for the winter. As our bedroom was unheated, we stored the winter squash under our beds. The logic of this is a bit vague, but they never spoiled, and I never had the nightmares about monsters under my bed that bedeviled other children. One year we raised blue hubbard, a large squash with a hard, blue-green rind and lacking any hint of symmetry. They were impossible to cut open. We resorted to an axe, but you still needed some device to hold this recalcitrant vegetable, else the axe blow just broke the skin and caromed off dangerously, like trying to cut down a hornbeam. I don't remember if we ever actually ate one.

More repetitive but less closely supervised was mowing. Equipment costs money, which was always in short supply, and our farm's size—three acres, including the brook—was too small for larger, labor-saving equipment. So we used what we had. Our Sears, Roebuck twenty-one-inch, five-horsepower push-mower was pressed into mowing the fields, almost two acres of them. We wanted the grass short, so predators could not then hide, and the birds could forage more easily. Round and round I went on a summer day, six miles an acre—

"Six miles? How'd you know six miles?"

"I figured it out, assuming a square, which it was not, and a cutting width of eighteen inches, which is generous."

"And you figured this out why?—"

"To be more engaging at parties. And figuring it out is more interesting than actually doing it."

—five miles a gallon, pushing the mower through heavy swale, down into ditches, over rocks. The mower sometimes fetched up on a hillock and stopped short with a grinding retch, but, having cleared it, it always started right up again. Couldn't break that mower. Hours were spent doing what a gang-mower on level ground could have done in minutes. The tortured machine never complained.

Berries grew along roads and stone walls and in fields, and picking them was one of those summer jobs that carried a suspiciously high level of parental approval. You learned to be suspicious of such "fun" things or of any job with an implied promise that "once done," you could go to town for the rest of the day. Parents promoted berry-picking as fun so as not to have to dragoon you into doing it anyway.

The first ripe were the strawberries. Forget the strawberries you know: these were smaller than a blueberry and easier to mangle than the liver of a young duck. A handful was as close to heaven as you were likely to get, unless, of course, you had a color TV. But you had to work for this theophany, on your knees, face pushing aside the tall grass, fingers pushing down into the thatch. A quart was a good hour's work in the field and nearly as much at the table, hulling them and picking out the straw and the green ones.

Of all the smells in the country, and there are many—just-picked wild strawberries, lilacs (who can smell lilacs and not want to be in love?), a horse's work harness, peonies, new-mown hay, burning leaves, making jam—the best remains that of laundry fresh off the line after a day in the bright sun. You want to bury yourself in the fluffy pile, to somehow ingest the air itself. Like an addict, each lung-full only produces the need for a more intense experience.

Blueberries, on their low bushes, were easier to pick and less prone to mushing. Our only source was a partially overgrown field reachable by walking through woods. It felt distant, slightly dangerous, since it opened on nothing familiar. Raspberries in August, blackberries in September. The amounts we brought home were modest, for we only picked from the patches along the road, the same patches available to others. Wild patches on private property were, by common consent, left alone; such patches might yield ten quarts in two hours. We accepted the inevitable scratches as a minor inconvenience. A torn shirt showed zealous courage. The thing most feared while forcing your way into the midst of a patch was stepping on a yellow jacket nest, as your ability to move quickly was highly compromised. Homemade raspberry pie was described reverently, the voice low and thick with emotion. Listeners wet their lips and moaned in agreement.

Part IV

David's Stories

As mentioned in the preface, these fictionalized incidents, as part of an effort to convert the whole piece to the third person, were the only ones that actually made the transition. "David" was my father's young alter ego, and, given the emotional dynamics on which these stories rest, most appropriately adopted here in Part IV.

Chapter XX

Squeezing Case

W hy's the table moved?" Jerry asked of no one in particular, since there was no one in the kitchen. His questions always had unpleasant harmonics, overtones of demand: if you are within the sound of my voice, pony up! They had just walked in. Through the back window David saw the school bus lurch away from Farnum's. The roar of its straining diesel faded quickly; the bus shrank to a furry yellow blob in the approaching twilight and then, somewhere near Fred Cunningham's, vanished.

School buses are made to make too much noise. What's to eat?

The kitchen smelled of disuse and a kerosene burner gone cold; coffee grounds lay in the open garbage. Some-Fun nosed open the back door and arched his back against David's leg, creating a caricature of neediness—shameless fawning, overenthusiastic purring. *I'm considering being your best friend. I will never play you false.* David wanted to believe: the universe awaited his considered reply. Footsteps coming down the steep attic stairs—the universe would have to wait.

His father comes in, preoccupied, and carrying a trouble-light, the one that Jerry wounded when he ran the saw into it in August.

What a relief it was to have him make a mistake once in a while.

The splice was bandaged with electrical tape, a black gall on the fat, orange cord. "Did you hear me? I said why's the table moved?"

"Maggots," his father blurts out, visibly uncomfortable with having to give up the details.

There's that motion of discomfort: hips tighten; shoulders rotate slightly.

———

"Maggots started dropping down on it through the light fixture—I was eating lunch—so I moved it. Something must have eaten the rat poison in the barn and got in somehow and died in the ceiling."

What'd he press him for? Can't he see he's upset?

Jerry never bothers to monitor the discomfort of others—or even his own: a kind of opaque cruelty that becomes a life-long habit. His father gets the DDT from under the sink. Again, the footsteps, going up. David watches his graham crackers circle listlessly in the now-contested airspace, stacked up over this unresolved mess, awaiting clearance from his brother, the air traffic controller of afterschool snacks.

There is, however, a value in distractions.

The forceful removal of a floorboard in the attic causes the ceiling tiles to emit a high haze of ancient dust, and the pace of drizzling maggots temporarily rises. From above, the periodic, diffuse scuffle of the electric cord dragging slowly behind the trouble-light. Disbelief explodes. "Oh, Christ! Oh, for Christ's sake . . . for Christ's sake!" Silence. Consideration. "Jerry, bring up that old table cloth that's on the little bookcase in the back hall."

The attic. Burlap bags of drying feathers hang scrotum-like from the rafters. The trouble-light dangles over the edge of the partially removed floorboard creating, between the exposed joists, a trough brimming with concentrated brightness. Pendulous shadows stagger across the unfinished roof. His father is on his knees shoving some boxes out of the way, stacking others—the detritus of former lives. Jerry attends, David watches. "Let me have that tablecloth—unfold it—spread it here," he says to Jerry. "Give me an edge—no—shiny side up." He opens his jackknife and cuts down the bag closest to him, handling it carefully. "Maggots," he adds, "the maggots are in the feathers." He hesitates before taking the first step on the often-traveled road of historical revisionism. "Did you notice anything last week?"

David feels a drop in the air pressure; his father's anger finds a hollow spot high up between his lungs and coils there like a snake, waiting. "They stink," he managed to say last Sunday after finishing. He came up here with his brother, and starting at the far end, they took down each bag and without untying it, shook around the contents. Palpating the bag to find the biggest clumps of feathers, they massaged them apart to speed drying—"squeezing case," wasn't that what his father called it, smiling at some private joke—and then hung it back up. They worked on their hands and knees—it was a filthy job. Every bag belched forth a face full of mites and feather dust. The dust of the feathers mixed with the dust of the floor; the single, naked light bulb floated in a yellow-brown haze. And now? How many maggot eggs . . . and what other stuff do they make? He shudders. The only redeeming aspect of this chore: it was the only chore of the day. They were free. Jerry treads carefully. "No, I didn't see anything." Level, apodictic. The question stands answered without David's confirmation.

The first load of infected bags, bundled in the old oilcloth, gets carried out back of the barn and unceremoniously dumped; the oilcloth returns for the second load and for the third. With such an awkward armful, the stairs require some negotiating: his father carries, David works the doors, Jerry spreads the table cloth and piles. The last load is small. "Take this out back of the barn, Jerry. I'm going to spray and then get the gas can. David, get the box of matches from the kitchen." They reassemble behind the barn.

The gasoline ignites explosively—*Kaa-aa-thuuunkkkk!* "Doesn't do very much," his father offers, sensing David's appreciation of the fireworks. "Burns too fast." The burlap glows for a moment, then ceases to exist. Freed of all constraints, softball-size clumps of feathers sag and break off, igniting as they tumble awkwardly to the ground.

If I had just gone up . . . if I had just gone up earlier and massaged the bags . . .

David considers the terrible judgment visited upon the maggots and finds little justification. Weren't they just doing their maggoty thing? His silent plea for mercy is answered by a swarm of angry maggots surging out of the *auto-da-fé*, filling his mouth, burning his lips, looking for their eggs.

"All show and no go," Jerry offers with the same high seriousness with which he might quote Cicero, unmindful that the context is of a different kind of fire. His father hesitates, shifts his weight. "Don't use that phrase. It means . . . it means . . . something sexual." The crackle of the pyre flows into an embarrassed silence. The stinking effluvia, awash in flame, sends a column of oily smoke into the evening sky. They leave it to burn itself out; the ground is too damp for the fire to spread. The old table cloth goes in the garbage, the final stop of its retirement.

"Snack time," David says, trying to speak with unopposable enthusiasm, afraid it wouldn't fly. It didn't.

"Chores," his father says, shortly, but without judgment. "Moms will be home soon."

Jerry was not to be left out of the child management program. "Yes, you need to get your chores done, and it's too close to supper. You'll ruin your appetite." The loss of hope created a vacuum; the loss of lift produced a chorus of insistent warning buzzers. He saw the night sky now glinting through tears, filled with endless flashing stall lights; the graham crackers, one after another, peeled off like P-38s from the *USS Hornet*, slipping sideways on one wing, trading altitude for speed, turning. Their wings flashed once, and then they were gone.

The headlights of the green Suburban turn into the driveway—Mom's home from school. They walk over. "My, such a welcoming committee!" David's mother says. "What's the fire I saw? Everything all right?"

His father explains how when they slaughtered that big load of ducks from the State Prison Farm in September, a sharp frost hadn't yet killed off the flies. These flies laid their eggs in the wet feathers which they then bagged up and took to the attic to dry. The eggs hatched into maggots that finally grew so numerous and so voracious that they ate through the burlap and so, onto the floor, through the cracks between the boards, into the light fixture and onto the kitchen table. She makes a face. "I'll be goddamned," he says, "if I didn't hear them chewing away inside the nearest bag when I leaned over to look under the boards with the trouble-light."

David's mother swings her legs out of the van, signaling the reassertion of necessity; the maggots have even then begun to drift into her past, where events are packed so tightly they are never reexamined. The welcoming committee scatters: Jerry to the back seat for her books and papers to grade, his father to the furnace, David to the evening chores. His mother changes into old clothes and starts constructing supper.

Finished with chores. Pails in the back hall for the morning, boots along the wall, bright lights in the kitchen. The sullen odor of the DDT tries to rein in the expansive, bright smell of re-warming spaghetti sauce but is ultimately unsuccessful. At supper, David's father revisits the intricacies of maggots and feathers, examining every possible branch in the road from the State Prison Farm ducks to the kitchen table maggots, considering the number of prison trustees who helped, the duration of each event, the weather, the burlap, the bushel baskets, the sequence of events, and the events themselves, and the checks from the Chicago Feather Co. that would never arrive. By dessert, he has produced a videotape of the whole sordid affair: in quiet moments, the massager of feathers can always head off the maggots. The check is in the mail.

Several years later, there was another maggot incident. The feathers, however, were not in the attic—they were, rather, in pillows that David's mother had stuffed with their own goose down. At some point on that night, his father figured out that the gentle rustle he heard when he put his head on his pillow was the sound of many small mouths. He leapt up in the dark with a roar of angry disgust, took the pillows downstairs, and threw them out the front door into the yard.

Chapter XXI

The Bus Ride

"U p Quimby!" A metallic, imperious shriek from Miss Mullen, the usual second-floor whip of the daily "get out of school" drill. The kids who walked home up Quimby Street hill were the first to be delivered.

A big-boned woman with fine hair on her face, she positioned herself strategically at the end of the hall. From there she could watch the progress of the same drill on the floor below. In those days, talking while in the hall was forbidden. David quailed before the sweep of her eyes, which passed over the children's heads like the beam of a prison searchlight, savaging those who talked or failed to keep up with wordless, feral intensity.

"Down Bangor!" Each classroom doorway, in turn, released its noisy shuffle so as to make one long line. They streamed toward the big, creaky wooden stairs, rubber boots clomping, mittens swinging, where Miss Mullen released them on seeing the tail of the first floor line pass below.

The bus kids were always last. The wait produced a pressure around David's heart—like holding his breath under water: the urgency building, dulling every other need but to seek relief. Finally their turn came, and he and the others and his brother up ahead trooped down the hall clutching dog-eared workbooks and clanking metal lunchboxes, clumped down the wide stairs and out into the schoolyard, which despite the fading afternoon sun and the cold and the snow, was a relief from the threat of the hallway's closed closet doors and their mysterious contents, from the oppressive classrooms with their desks rigidly bolted down to the floor, a relief from the close smell of wet wool and rubber and pine oil cleaner in the closets, of pencil-sharpener shavings and orange rinds in the wastebaskets, and of old arithmetic books in the desks.

On better days, he joined a gang and paraded around the snowy, trampled playground, displaying camaraderie manufactured strictly for the moment, or played in some noisy game, or successfully avoided the playground teachers for a couple of quick snowballs. Discussions of the outside world centered around Chevrolets and Fords and television: what was on last night, what was on tonight, what their fathers watched. Fortunes were to be had by certain knowledge of those worlds, worlds in which David felt bankrupt. The short afternoons were a whirl of friendships made, unmade, and made again.

Their bus lumbered around from its first run, and the door flopped open with the limberness of the closet door in a cheap motel room. The lineup for the bus, the shoving, yelling, cursing, the metallic smell of the bus's interior mixed with that of crumpled waxed paper and apple cores. The driver was pleasant and talkative, with a ruddy, slack-jawed face and a big, ready smile. At Christmas time John drove with a huge can of rock candy near the door, expecting everyone to help themselves as they got out. David felt being near such a friendly man a rare pleasure. In the spring, he'd play marbles with the older kids. Sitting near enough to watch the action was exciting: marbles changing hands, the lead seesawing back and forth. In response to the challenge of "How many?" John would cast an eye at the white-knuckled, grubby paw, flash his easy grin at the kid to kind of size him up, roll easily in the seat, look in the mirror, check the road, throw the big, black-armed, gear-shift lever into third, blink once and say, "Three." He won uncomfortably often. "Hubba-hubba!" he exclaimed, and the bus roared away down the black stretch of salt-stained road.

David got on the bus late. All the seats near John were taken, and he started his way back through a gauntlet of noisy, lying nose-pickers. He looked up the aisle and prayed for a friend in an open seat or for an invitation; even sitting with his brother was better than sitting next to someone uninvited: he dreaded the howls of protest or the feigned objections or the derision normally reserved for Nash Ramblers. No friends, few open seats. Not Mary Blodget again! Last week he had had to sit with her: "Fat Mary," the kids called her. Calls of "Who's your friend?" broke over his head and drained slowly down his neck. He had ridden with stiffened body, gazing intently at the person's haircut in front of him. But now?—quick, what other choices? Only Michael Pinkman— sometimes a friend, often an abusive bully.

In the winter there were no marbles, and he rode intensely aware that he was not part of the surrounding noisy mêlée. The patrol boy stood up in front of the bus wearing the coveted symbols of his authority: the white belt and the silver badge. His job: cranking open the bus door by the big shiny handle, checking traffic when kids had to cross the road, attempting to keep some order. What ease! What confidence!

The houses along the way—what Edens lay behind the curtains of those homes? What warmth and comfort? "Would they like me?" David wondered. Every part of the way was so familiar, the land a complex fabric, the views, the icy rock outcroppings, the traffic-tarnished banks of snow which turned pristine only a short distance into the unsullied fields, the mysterious forests of pine, the apple trees which in the fall held promise of rich reward for those bold enough try. The trip home— always the same road—was familiar and predictable. Always the same road, yet never the same trip, and ever to be travelled in different degrees of attention, of reverence, moods changing from place to place, now near an unknown patch of woods, now near the house of a friend, now by a house where there were no kids, making the place forbidding and unknowable, now near the place of some unmentionable sin.

Left on South Belfast Avenue.

The kids start to get off, singly, in small clumps, in noisy gangs. See ya' tomorrah, Ray; Yeah, see ya'. My fatha got two deah this year. He did not! Oh yeah? Whada' you know? Think ya' know everythin'? Yer fatha get a deah? His fatha didn't even get a deah! Blue suede shoes 'cause my motha she works at Hazard, gets 'em real cheap. My fatha's gonna get my brotha a real good job this summa downta the mill. Teacha, she's gonna call my old lady, says I'm actin' up all the time, bitch.

A prickle of fear sweeps the listeners.

Gonna buy me a new glove this spring Peggy! Peggy! What'sah matta? What'sah matta? Break it in like the pros.

The bus heavy with the smell of wet wool and partially-eaten lunches.

I'm gonna make a caht with a ol' lawn-mowa engine. You ain't neither—you said that last year! Ya wanna bet? Wanna bet I ain't? My brotha's gonna help me!

Left on Church Hill Road.

SIDOWN BACK THERE! Ya know that long rope we got in the barn—that really long one? my brother he hooked it up way up on the top rafter in the barn—swing and drop into the hay! I wonder if I can get her alone to continue. See ya, Al and that lucky big hole in her pocket. See ya. Secret feel deep. A passing slap. I'll git ya tomorrah, ya bastid, see if I don't and ya ain't neva gonna ride on my caht! Kin I have a ride. Ya got nose trouble, kid? turn around, ya dink! Ah va, you said a dirty word; I'm gonna tell Mumma when we git home! Don't you dare tell! I will so! You tell and I'll punch you good—you tell and I'll tell everyone about youknowwhat. No! Not that! I gotta git see ya. And Bring yer stuff tomorrah. See ya Andy. Comin' ovah to watch TV tonight? Kin I? Sure, after suppa. I'll ask my fatha if I kin come. GET YER HEAD OUTTA THAT WINDOW! He uses double-bladed skates. Dumbo, dumbo! We was at the camp last summer fishing and a pickerel bit my uncle's hand. They have teeth? Billy Owens got a brown ring around . . . You ain't never seen a pickerel?

Across North Belfast Avenue.

One way goes into town, the other to the distant reaches of Maine, strange and unimaginably far. The bus is emptier.

Gordons

get off and trudge toward their house in the early evening twilight.

Bowmans—

sitting with a friend, trying. Alone.

Heallys—

and the uneasiness of approaching. A kind of death.

Saunders—

home starts to grow. Will everything be all right?

Hendersons—

will the ducks and geese be running around? Maybe the kids'll laugh. I hope everything—

Turcottes—

I hope the old car is not in the driveway. I hope—

Farrell's—

will my father be outside?

Mollisons—

maybe the driver could go right by and then come back after everyone was let off and let me and my brother off and then,

embarrassed no one would see,

maybe I could ride forever, an entire lifetime spent looking out the window, the bus rocking on its unforgiving springs, banging on the potholes and sweeping down the hill and one glance and whew! everything is OK and it brakes hard, slow, slow, stop. David follows his brother down the long aisle, three steps, two steps, one step and made it! no comments into the cold. The door cranks shut, the bus, covered to the windows with salt and road dirt, roars off.

Why does he always go so slow? Can't he get it out of here quicker so no one'll see?

Safely away now, past the bridge.

Across the road, the mailbox noses out warily from the embankment of packed snow. The house is dark and uninviting. David walks to the back porch, where Jerry, having just finished sweeping the snow off his boots, hands him the broom. "Here you are, dawdler. You must have been enjoying the weather."

The white kerosene drums, mute and crowned with a ridge of snow, lie heavily on their wooden racks. The house feels hollow, the air strained. His father, as always, comes into the kitchen to say, "Hello. How are you? How's school? What did you do today?"—then disappears back into his study.

"Hey, that's too much jam," Jerry objects, just loudly enough for his father to hear, but not so loudly to be judged a disturbance. David and his brother bicker over who gets the funnies from the *Daily Kennebec Journal* first, how many graham crackers are enough, how much jam is enough.

It was many years before I actually had some graham crackers; back then I only ate them.

David's turn for the funnies finally came. He liked to read them toasting his toes with the smoky furnace heat of the living-room register. The comics were too short, and the funny ones not very funny. The beauty of comics is that the characters exist only in the action; they have no place. He read *Major Hoople* because his father read it, meaning it must be clever and funny: he never got it; *Mark Trail*, good-looking, resourceful, ever in love, always gets through; *Rip Kirby, PI*, handsome, notices the details, always gets his man (and the woman); *Captain Easy* streaks through the universe, solving problems on alien worlds.

David thought about what problems he could solve—the list was short, the objections many, the revisions endless.

Time for chores before it gets dark. David retrieves his boots from the back hall and noses them under the stove to thaw. Three gas burners on high for two pots plus the big tea kettle. Water from the priming can gurgles down the pump's throat, wetting its leather sinuses. Suction. Refill the priming can, fill the teakettle, haul it out of the black cast-iron sink and onto the stove.

Don't drip, please.

Quick! Grab the first pot and fill it before the pump loses its vacuum—the gently-curved handle clanks, the water, soft and splashy, rolls off the jutting spout which flares like the prognathous lower jaw of a baboon. Haul the pot. On the stove. Next pot. Done.

Upstairs, this morning's frost flowers still cover the bottom half of the inside of their bedroom window. He hangs up his school clothes, comes down and goes into the back hall with its smells of tired wool, stale coats, and the inside of galoshes. Last night's cold had nested deep inside his chore clothes and could only be driven out by sacrificing body heat. He shivers. He chances another minute of furnace heat from the floor radiator—the big pots are not yet boiling—a minute that risks censure for stalling. Having reread *Mark Trail*, who had just found his way to safety from the icy reaches of the Klondike, David grabs the steaming tea kettle, slides into his boots, and heads for the barn. Hit the lights. The cavernous space overwhelms the single dusty bulb to which adhere, randomly, the abandoned body parts of moths. Pull chain by the grain barrels. Into the duck house. Another light.

He uses the hot water judiciously

not too much, now!

to free each pail from the floor's icy grip, taking each newly-freed pail into the yard and gently whacking—

easy!—

it on an old piece of six-by-six lying there, and by using the balance of the hot water as necessary dumps out the icy block.

He makes a halfhearted attempt to clean the bottoms of the pails and leaves them in the barn. Back to the house. Grab this morning's pails from the back hall.

Scrape your boots, please!

Tracking duck shit into the house is frowned upon. Into the kitchen. The water is now very hot. David divides the hot water from the pots among the three pails, tops each off with cold water, and stages them into the back hall. In the failing light, the gas dryer appears a ghostly white shrine. First pail to the barn. Close the house door behind you— don't waste heat. Back for the second.

Don't slosh it—keep it away from your legs!

Three pails necessitate three trips. Now into the duck house—each pail needs a fresh spot—anywhere but in one of the established donuts, which, by cleaning time on the weekend, would dot the floor like so many messy calderas.

Back to the barn. Tops off the feed barrels. Make sure to use a feed bucket, not a water bucket. Half a bucket of pellets; another half of corn. His arrival with the bucket of grain establishes him firmly in the minds of the inhabitants as a real prince of a guy, the proof of which is a cacophonous greeting and widespread disappearance of any fear, being perfectly willing to run over your boots on their way to the food.

Leave now, like Joe DiMaggio, while you are at the height of your popularity.

Shut the duck-house light and lock the door. Back into the barn, drop the grain pail on top of the others, cover the barrels. Pull chain. Barn light.

He liked to roll the barn door shut. He liked its satisfying impact, its organic power—timber against timber, its blank disdain. What momentum it had, once you got it rolling—what irresistible momentum! or was it moment of inertia? He could never keep them straight. He stepped out into the cold.

It was useless, what he had just done. Just another kind of dark.

He considered putting his back against the door frame, in front of the in-rushing door, the heavy in-rushing door, bearing the weight of all the lost graham crackers and the weight of the useless shadow that he threw, always growing away from the light. He wanted to be near the light and cast a shadow. His father would know how to do that. A sharp heave on the bolted rigidity of the steel handle. The screech of the steel wheels rolling their pursed lips along the overhead track. Thud! Oh, the pails, he forgot the goddamned pails!

Scrape your boots, please.

The winter chores done, it's homework time or practicing time or reading time or looking-through-the-Sears-Catalog time. The kerosene tank tunk-tunks melodiously; the logs in the furnace clunk and sigh as they are consumed. The house hunches, the inhabitants quiet, isolated, related only by common anticipation.

Headlights coming down the road, seen through the frosty window, across the bridge, slowing.

"There's Mom's," his father would say, brightening. He gets up from his chair and paces ritually into the kitchen for a swallow of lukewarm coffee. The front porch light is turned on as welcome. David pulls on his boots again and goes out to help carry in the groceries; Jerry gets the armful of workbooks and papers she will dutifully correct. His mother's cheery voice. Everyone is pleased at seeing her and having her home. David's father goes out to put the car away for the night. The kitchen bustles; dinner is on the stove. For David, sitting on the tall wooden stool, the late winter afternoon glows.

Chapter XXII

Crows Are Like That

Augusta Spring 1960

The wind came full south, and the pall of smoke sluggishly wore away, straight at the church. The man in the distance moved in a frenzy, now trying to contain the spreading grass fire with the club-end of a straw broom, now running into the blackened semicircle waving and yelling, now starting to run toward the road, only to halt after a few steps and return to the fire, whose very deliberateness mocked his desperation and indecision. The burnt area grew slowly, like a fiery-edged moon eclipsing a sun of frost-bleached grass.

She was working as she always worked, in a gentle haze of preoccupation. The cries from the other side of the brook finally leaked into the present, into the chore of the moment: washing the kitchen floor. One look out the back window and she went to the phone. "Go help your father!" she called to Jerry out the front door. "Where's

David? Get David! Get a broom or a shovel! Tell him I called the fire department! Run!"

Jerry dropped the rake and ran, skipping over the piles of dead plants dotting the garden. David, off to one side and screened by the maple that flared up in a shuttlecock of small trunks, being closer to the barn, got there first. He grabbed the push broom.

"No, not the push broom! It'll burn. Get the snow shovel," Jerry ordered. They ran down the road. Seeing help on the way, the firefighter gave up his painful antics and concentrated on the edge of the fire closest to Gilley's.

They worked as a team around the fire's perimeter: Jerry scraped the flames into the already blackened circle, thus depriving the fire of fresh fuel; David followed a few steps behind, doing flare-up control. Every movement caused grey dust to boil up from the burnt grass; the smoke stung his sweaty face. "We're doing good . . . we're going to get it," David chanted, as they started to arc back toward their property. The dangerous direction of the fire had been checked.

"Let me have your shovel for a while, bub," his father said. The tool exchange promised no glory: his shovel for a blackened broom, now no bigger than a toilet plunger, and the half-empty pail of water which his father had gotten from the brook. "You're on flare-up patrol." Jerry followed his father back around the circle.

Only thin, sour smoke greeted the fire truck when it arrived. It swung up Gilley's driveway; the crew swarmed out to their preassigned tasks. Two of them grabbed the end of a hose and started dragging it toward the ponded water behind the dam. A third attached the end of the same hose to the large, shiny water intake and then walked around the truck to start uncoiling a smaller hose with a brass nozzle. The three others heaved Indian pumps onto their backs, grabbed their long-handled McLeods, and walked to the edge of the still-smoldering grass. They worked their way around the perimeter of the blackened circle, alternately dousing an area with water from their pumps and then thoroughly raking it over.

"Thanks for coming so fast," his father said, smiling ruefully at his own clumsy indiscretion.

"Not a problem," the crew chief answered with a hint of mechanical politeness. "I need some information for my report. You were trying to burn off the grass?" The question was perfunctory: he could see the recently burned fields across the brook.

"Yes. There's only a small piece of my property on this side of the brook. The wind was out of the west, and I thought I could handle it. But the wind shifted, and the grass was drier than I thought."

They walked to the truck to continue. The boys watched the crew re-coil their heavy hoses and swing their pumps onto the rack. There was an old Indian pump in the barn—a smaller version. He liked to squirt it, but not to carry it: the narrow straps bit into his shoulders, and the uncompromising, naked metal of the tank pressed on his back. "How much do they hold?" he ventured.

"Six gallons—heavy. You wouldn't have some drinking water around, would you?" Jerry offered to go to the house and bring some back. "Naw, don't bother; we're almost done."

The several cars and trucks that had stopped to watch the excitement drove off. Pearl Cunningham had heard the yelling also and had summoned Ernest from the barn; John Trask stopped on his way to town; Allen Farnum, who lived just on the other side of the church, had come running over.

The truck swung in a wide circle, just intersecting with the blackened grass, and shouldered its way back across the field and down the driveway. They were gone. Ernest stayed behind to talk. "You okay, Henry?"

"Ya, sure, just feeling stupid."

"Wind come around on ya', didn't it?"

"Ya, it sure did."

Ernest swung over to us. "You boys gonna help me next summer?—be good money!"

He and his brother answered differently, but together, "Ya, sure . . . oh, yes . . . we're gonna help you."

The thought that they might be able to say no had not yet occurred to either.

His father picked up the snow shovel. "So long, Ernest; thanks for stopping by."

"Sure, so long Henry. How's the missus?"

"She's fine, thanks."

We started walking toward the road, Jerry with the bucket, I with the remains of the old broom with its unruly nub of grey straw.

A car came down the hill slowly and pulled over. "That's George," his father said. "The fire trucks must have passed him when he was already on the road."

"Why'd he take so long to get here then?"

"Don't know. He must've stopped at home for some reason—groceries, or Mildred was with him." His father went over to talk. David and his brother waved hello and started up the road.

* * *

On another fall day, several years later, they had walked across the plank bridge—just David and his father—up the slope and across the field toward the small crowd milling around a dead deer hanging from a tree, a large tree and remarkable for being the only tree on the Gilleys' property not part of the actual woods which started at the back of their field. They were selling the place. The fall leaves, before the inevitable leaching rains of early winter, were ablaze: clumps of color marched away in every direction like processions of medieval gonfalons; between them the fields were sun-covered wagons carrying pumpkins and acorns, wagons piled with carelessly-tied bundles of corn stalks and drawn by drooling oxen with angular bodies; the occasional pines small marching bands of cornets and trombones; somewhere a bass drum thumped. Else only the unblemished sky above, hard and impenetrable, the sharp stubble crunching underfoot, and the crows.

"Crows always try to get behind me; from every new perch they watch and are never satisfied," David thought. "Crows are like that." The crows and the sky and the dead deer and over all the fugitive noonday warmth—the land rang with the last hours of Indian summer. Frank Sr. walked over. "Hi, Henry." He spoke with a wheezing rattle.

"Hi-ya Frank. Good to see you. Who shot the deer?"

"Frankie got him near dark yesterday. Nice weather we're havin'. How's the missus? She still teachin'?"

"She's fine, thanks. Yeah, she's still at Vassalboro—they made her the principal."

"Is that so? Is that so? Well, she sure deserves it. My niece and nephew both had her—you remember Don Haskell, don't you?—his kids—they both had her in seventh and eighth grade, ya' know, and both of 'em are now in college."

"Is that so? Well, that's very nice to hear. Say hello to Elaine when you see her." David vaguely remembered her—she had come over for tutoring in math. David envied her—her confidence, her varsity jacket, and the hour of good-natured patience from his father.

"I will, I will. They still speak of her teaching, ya' know. Where's your other boy?"

"Jerry's at a private school in New Hampshire called Exeter. He got a scholarship. He'll be home next week." His father slid his hand into the waistband of his pants. Seth Foster drove by and honked. The compass of the talk swung easily on the gimbals of the warm afternoon. "Had any offers on the house?"

"A couple, but not enough money, ya' know."

"If you don't mind telling me, how much are you asking for the place?"

"Twenty-one."

"Is that so? That much, huh?"

The pitch of his wheezing rose slightly. "Well, it ain't so much—remember I got 107 acres—107 acres clear back half way to Togus Pond, ya' know, and it ain't been cut in over 70 years or better, long before I was born. And then I got a drilled well—210 feet they went."

"That much land? I didn't know. Well, good luck with it, I wish you the best." David's father swung slightly toward the deer. "Nice looking buck." Frankie Junior's trophy was hanging by its horns from a low limb. They wandered over. Hardened blood covered its face and stippled its sides. A chill settled on the afternoon. Frankie and several older friends, or maybe they were cousins, were getting ready to load the deer into their truck and take it to the tagging station. Warren Stone stood near them. David risked a wave and a smile.

"Did you shoot it in the head?" David asked Frankie, feeling exposed and unfortunately ignorant, like when he had asked his father if he knew what a madeleine was.

"You must be a hell-uv'a shot!" grinned Warren, poking fun by way of teasing Frankie.

Henry and Muriel, Vassalboro schoolyard.

"No, I got him through the lungs." David imagined the panting deer plunging wounded through the underbrush, while with every breath great bubbles of blood burst out of its nose.

David eased himself out of the group around the deer and swung over to where Allen and—and who?—were standing. David didn't recognize him. "Another cousin probably—looks older," thought David. Jim Robinson turned out to be from Randolph.

"Well, did you go?" David asked. They had talked about it Friday waiting for the bus. "Did you go down there Friday night?" Even though he didn't want to know the details, he knew better than not to ask—part of standard teenage protocol to fend off the taunts of being queer.

"Naw, my uncle and his family came over for a barbecue, and I couldn't just walk away from my cousins. But we did go down there on Saturday."

"Where is 'there,'" Jim asked.

Allen pointed diagonally to a field across the road. "And you see that road?—you can just see the end—they drive down to the bottom of the hill and then turn into the field."

"Oh, okay, so it's not all driving across the fields in the dark?"

Allen assured him that they all used the road. "So you and Stevie?—"

"Yeah. My parents went over to some party at my father's boss's house—I think his daughter got married yesterday—and I told 'em I was going to Stevie's to watch television."

"How many cars were there?" The two of them had gone down to the bottom of the field across the road, down to where the guys "parked," and crept up on the cars to listen to what the occupants were doing. It was inconceivable to me that I could be part of that world.

"Three—no two when we first got there. Then another one came. We almost got caught in the headlights. We never got near it, anyway, 'cause the moon rose and we had to get out of there. And it was gettin' late, and I didn't want my parents to see Stevie walking home when we were supposed to be at his house." Stevie lived in the other direction, over on Stevens Road. "The couple in the first car got into an argument, but the second car—they were screwin'. You should'a heard the moaning and the springs in the seat!"

Someday I will find out all about screwing, as long as I don't have to talk about it with anyone. To relieve myself of the difficulty in seeing these primal scenes I take a box cutter and draw it slowly down my arm, being careful to stay between the tendons.

———

David shuffled awkwardly. "Yeah. We saw that couple once—" he ventured. An old story, but something appropriate to fill the space.

"Oh, yeah. Tell me about that time again—Jim hasn't heard this story—the time you saw that couple—"

"Yeah. We were haying down by the first bridge." He pointed again for Jim's benefit. "Further down that same road."

"Who was in the rack again?"

"I don't really remember. Jerry and Ernest, certainly. And there they were, stretched out on a blanket, and here we come, the old rack creaking and pitching down the slope of the field behind the old house, the breeching straps tight up against Tommy's thighs—I think they were surprised to see us."

"Weren't they doin' anything?"

"No, I don't think so. He didn't have any of her clothes off yet." He blushed and stopped—he had never really looked. "Next day, Ernest stopped the truck and we got out and found the spot. He just had to go investigate."

"There they were," he had said with obvious relish, pointing to the matted-down grass and, curling his tongue around the corner of his mouth, added, "grassin', they was grassin'."

David saw his father turn to go. "See you tomorrah, Allen. Gotta go." He caught up with this father by the brook. Nearing home, the age-old tightness of unresolved conflict settled over them like a noxious cloud, stiffening their gait and making conversation difficult.

"They still speak of her teaching," isn't that what he said? "They still speak of her." David felt proud of the recognition but sensed it was rather too little—way too little. They knew nothing about her or her accomplishments, which were tightly packed away in a past rarely visited. And people were always speaking about her when she wasn't there. Why didn't anyone ever speak of her when she was there and in front of a room full of people?

"What are you doing now?"

"Practicing. And some homework. And I have to write a paper about a poem—I hate writing about poems. They're about what they say. What can you add?" David's speech was from higher up in his lungs, as if air was in short supply.

"What poem?"

"*Birches, After Apple-Picking*, or *Mending Wall*. We can pick. I think I'll pick *Mending Wall.*"

"Don't be fooled by its apparent simplicity—Frost is a master at conning you into not paying attention."

"Conning is right," David thought. "And I'm a master at not paying attention."

"I've got to reclaim some wax," his father said, turning into the little yard in front of the slaughterhouse.

David walked on.

Chapter XXIII

The Last Picture Show

She wanted to see them, had wanted to see them since last year. David had dragged his feet, had put her off, had agreed with no intention of complying—one of the pleasant fictions allowed married people—saying yes and meaning no, and never getting called for it. But this evening he felt that drill was wearing thin, despite her seemingly endless goodwill. Enough. Resigned, he went to the basement and came up with a box and his old, black briefcase.

"Oh! Are those the pictures?"

For him, time had drained away their immediacy, and the intervening years made it a chore to restore their original, organic vitality or to communicate the reason for having saved them at all. Bloodless images. Freeze-dried relationships. His world slipping away. His world. His world? Did he ever have it?

Studebaker, Center Montville.

Barn in Center Montville.

"Yeah." David opened the briefcase.

"So, what've you got here? What's this a picture of?"

"Why'nt you just look at the pictures without me?"

"Because until you put some flesh on them, give them a context, they lack dimension—like raw facts before they are explained and put in some order. I mean, how are they connected to you?"

"Okay. That's the house in Center Montville about fifteen years after we moved away. Still in pretty good shape, even though no one was living in it at the time. It's now ready for the bulldozer—partly because it was later owned for many years by a crazy woman. Now owned by some

Trough from the spring. Vicky Broder, Jeremy, Peter Webster. Center Montville, 1946.

Peter Webster, Jeremy, Vicky, Hugh. Center Montville 1946

people in Massachusetts, I think."

"Who are these people?"

"My cousin Toria and her husband from New York. She spent at least one and maybe two summers up here and had a certain fondness for the place, so she wanted to go back for a visit."

"That their car?"

"No, that was my first car: a 1953 Studebaker Commander with

Up the road.

Up towards Ernest's, fall 1966.

overdrive. Ran okay—some body rot— And that's a picture of the barn."

"Big, 'ol barn. That's where you hid during the blasting?"

"Yes."

"This is you and your brother. Who's the black kid?"

"No, that's not me, that's Toria. Peter something-or-other. Parents were friends of my parents, I guess, and they sent him up for the summer—and also paid for him to be there. If I didn't have the picture,

Hugh and Jeremy.

Jeremy and Hugh

I wouldn't have remembered him at all— And there we all are near the front porch."

"And this? This is not the same house."

"No, that's Augusta. In the winter—looking across the brook. You can see my grandfather's house, and just beyond it, the slaughterhouse— And that's Ernest's house up the hill— And that's West Washington. What a dump."

"It looks like a dump. And this is you and your brother? You look like a couple of refugees from the Dust Bowl. The goats yours?"

"Yes, we had a few goats. I think they must have made the trip from Center Montville— That's still West Washington—my mother— And her one-room schoolhouse, later converted to a house."

Muriel. School yard. West Washington, 1948

Hugh and Jeremy

"God! Real rural poverty. Who's this?"

"That's Ernest Cunningham. Seventy years old. Out haying."

"Oh, and this is you on the hay rake. Terrible posture—didn't you have any bones?— And this is you and your brother with the ducks and geese?— And this is some sort of camp picture?"

"Yes. New England Music Camp. Another sacrifice to the god of music—again, not one redeeming moment. I showed little talent—what

Schoolhouse, West Washington. Later converted to a house.

Hugh on rake.

was I doing there? I guess my mother's need was so great that her usual brilliant, clear-eyed analysis failed her. She wanted me out in front of the orchestra playing the first movement of the Boccherini Cello Concerto—not Danny—Kowolski? Koblonski?—no, sounds too Polish—I don't

Henry and Muriel next to mobile home.

Ernest Cunningham, Augusta, 1957

remember. I should have gone to a camp for libido development."

"No sex there?"

"No, they had a really restrictive policy—to keep everyone focused on music, I guess. I don't think we were allowed to hold hands—and at dances, nose-to-nose was as close as you could get. And that was closer than I got."

"Whoa! Who's this, a hooker?"

"No, that's Dietzer something-or-other—Geffen maybe? A girlfriend. But that's what her friends said: 'She should'a been a hooker'— That's Albuquerque already. Outside their mobile home on New York Avenue."

"This is you with your cello. So arty! This was taken by a professional?"

"Actually, yes: my uncle, John Mills Sr. A professional photographer by training and avocation— That's us with our cousins

Hugh, Rochester, 1961. © John Mills

Jeremy, Hugh, Monument Beach, 1945

at Reid State Park. This was August, and the water was still colder than hell— That's at Monument Beach on Cape Cod. Before we moved to Maine."

"You were so good looking!"

"Yes. But it was wasted on me, alas— Here I am with my grandfather in Augusta—I suppose I was eighteen. All the chubbiness is gone, and now I look like Tom Cruise—but I'm taller."

"In your dreams!"

"No, I was. I told you the story about closing my office up in Belfast in 2008—"

"Remind me again about it."

"I put out the usual photocopied signs with my name and the office address and some of the stuff for sale. A couple comes upstairs—he asks

Camp at Kenab Creek.

Hugh with Zaide.

if I remember him from the State Highway Commission. I confess to having no memory. Then his wife asked me if I remember going out in a boat on a lake with someone named Carol—double date, I guess. I don't remember Carol, either. The woman reported that after the date, Carol

said I was the handsomest man she had ever been out with. What a waste."

"Okay, nice story. This is you?"

"That's me hiking in the Grand Canyon. I told you about making several long trips there—this is from the first one— And these are more pictures from my trips."

"Beautiful scenery. Where is this?"

"That's Kenab Creek Canyon, way off the beaten path—not even in the official national park. I camped there. There's the picture of my little space—I camped there

Jeremy and Hugh, end of shed.

for three days and only saw some mountain goats. Really remote. If you walk up the canyon far enough, assuming you could get out of it, you would be in Utah— That's Hermit's Creek—you can see the way it cut this amazing, narrow channel through the limestone— And that's me, coming back from Surprise Valley."

"What are you looking at?"

"The narrow trail I had just come over—you can see the narrow, sloping shelf of loose scree and dirt—carrying a heavy pack. One slip and you'd be dead—you'd roll half way to the river."

"And you were by yourself?"

"Well, not always, obviously, but yes, I guess I've always been a loner."

"What is this wreck? Looks like a mother's nightmare."

Hugh sweeping porch.

"That's Augusta when we first moved in. We knocked down the old shed between the house and the barn. If we look a little neglected there, it's because my mother was sick. You can see that I haven't had a haircut in about three months."

"This is Augusta again?"

"Yes. Sweeping the porch— And that's a picture of the family and me clowning around— My parents outside the backdoor— And here the shed is still standing. You can see our Model A Ford."

"Still looks good. How old was it?"

"Let's see, last made

Hugh looking back at trail.

in 1932 or maybe it was 1931, so eighteen or nineteen years old. I rode in the rumble seat several times. I believe it was a convertible—we had the top down at least once because I remember it."

"But I thought he sold his car in California during that awful trip out there?"

"He did, but that was back in the 1930s. He wrote that he asked $75 and ended up taking $55. It was this model, but not this car. He must have bought this one with money earned from gauge making—after all, it was wartime, and you could work just about as much overtime as you wanted—

That's Augusta: one of the bridges we made over the brook— That's Jerry home from Exeter, 1958 maybe— That's when they were in Spain, around 1965."

"This is the army?"

"Yes, that's Thailand. Some kind of company party in which we ended up throwing the company commander into the overflow pool at the water point—such drunken nonsense— That's out in the field in Germany—getting dressed outside my little pup tent— And that's Thailand again—the steel replacement of the famous bridge on the Kwai River— More Thailand—they're big on Buddha's— More Grand Canyon. Sunset. North Rim all

Augusta, 1952

The First Bridge, Augusta, 1958

lit up— Thunder River on the Tapeat's Trail."

"Another girlfriend? A horse woman?"

"Another girlfriend. Horseback riding in Albuquerque. We were engaged briefly. I took her to Albuquerque. She took me to Virginia or

Augusta, 1954

Family, Hugh clowning.

someplace. Her parents thought I was there to approve of them! The thought never entered my head, and, anyway, I was taught never to make judgments about people, so how could I evaluate anything?"

"So you had some girlfriends—I don't see what the problem was. And then there was that Andrea woman for

Jeremy home from Exeter.

whom you essentially moved to New York. And then Carolyne on 32nd St. that you liked so much. By the way, did you ever go through with getting your DNA checked to see if you were the father of Andrea's baby?"

"Yes, I sent in a sample. The test rejected the possibility of paternity in the 99.99 percentile. It was a Thomas Hardy moment."

"What's a Thomas Hardy moment?"

"Hardy's lead character always does something unfortunate at the

Henry, Jeremy, Hugh. Augusta, 1950

With Model A Ford.

beginning of the story—and he convinces himself (it was sometimes a woman) that he has successfully buried it. But Fate takes over—it comes to light at the end and bites him or ruins his life or exposes him as a criminal. In this case her daughter, after a search of fifteen years or so and now a mother herself, tracked down her birth mother."

"How'd she find that out?"

"When you turn eighteen, the adoptive agency has to give you the name of your birth mother, but obviously no bio. And then she tracked me down. But it was no fair. She knew someone who had access to national databases—could have gone to the police, as she told me she had police in her family—and then been bounced to God knows what federal database full of personal information. And so I get a letter—hand addressed but strangely without a zip code—on an island off the coast of Maine: 'I've found my mother and I'm looking for the other half of the equation.' Right out of Thomas Hardy."

"Okay, but back to women. You seem to have had plenty of girlfriends. You got married. You had three children. I don't understand . . ."

"The relationships were never light, just enjoy, just be . . . Instead, they were loaded, they existed in a haze of obligation, the women were way too important, sex was ponderous and then, eventually, perfunctory,

Hugh in Germany.

and then, inevitably, boring, and the kicker was that many of them liked me, and how could I tell a woman who liked me to take a hike, I'm just here for fun? These relationships had no freeboard, to use a nautical metaphor, and were constantly in danger of being swamped by their own importance."

"I think I understand. But with me its different, right?"

"Oh, of course."

"Ah, this is the famous class picture?"

"Yes, that's my seventh grade."

"You remember any of these people? Who's this?"

"Dick Merwin—lived on a farm out towards South China. Like Ray Andrews on our road, he smelled faintly of manure. He clomped around in rigid, square-toed ski boots all winter—such footwear was cool—only one level down from the coolest: white wool socks and moccasins."

"Moccasins in the deep snow?"

"Hey, cool is cool. He was always talking baseball cards. I didn't save them, so when I bought baseball gum I gave the cards to him. He once brought Whitey Ford's 1950 rookie card to school—claimed it was worth $150.

"That's John Cox. He was the most talented kid in the school— well, maybe Louis was, but John could sing all the latest songs, and they sounded just like the records. And he had so much confidence—not afraid to sing in front of the whole class. He brought his electric guitar to

Henry and Muriel, Spain, 1966.

school once. He was in Chizzle Wizzle, of course."

"What on earth was Chizzle Wizzle?"

"Four days of madness at Cony every year. Two days of a minstrel show—with an interlocutor and everybody in blackface."

"Blackface?"

"Yup. Hard to believe at this distance. Cony changed the rules shortly after my years there. Third night was an orchestra concert sandwiched between the acts of a play—or maybe they were back to back. The fourth night was the Chizzle-Wizzle Ball."

"You ever go to the Ball?"

"Maybe. I went to some prom. Ah, death, where were you? Anyway, John's mother was a crossing guard on Quimby. On rainy days, I could always tell it was her: instead of a raincoat she wore a bright yellow poncho with a picture of Goofy on the back."

"So you can dance?"

"No, can't dance. I can't move my body with enough abandon—too sexualized an activity—and you're on display, which means for sure I won't. I mean fast dancing—I can shuffle around to *Love Me Tender*."

"Shuffle reminds me of that slogan 'If you shuffle, you'll deal.' You ever do drugs?"

"Some pot. You could buy it off the street for pennies in Thailand. Overdosed on hash once—came down convinced I was a breach baby. I asked my mother. She said no. But the best experience was amphetamines. We were at some club in Bangor. A friend gave it to me. I started to talk— first time in my life I was actually voluble—this was about two a.m. I talked for the rest of the night, then drove home, kept talking, went visiting up the hill—kept talking— Don's father thought at first I was drunk, but then couldn't figure out what I was on. I finally stopped talking, and went to bed. I could have become an addict. I felt really alive. That's it."

"That's nothing compared to most people your age. Who's this?"

"That's Robert Harvey: short and strong. Had a birthmark covering his left ear that ran into his hair. Mimicked Richard Boucher's—that's him—speech behind his back. You know—that French-Canadian English with the rising intonation, making everything sound like a question? I saw him once in a while at our house because his sister took piano lessons from my mother. I remember he was in front of me in line one Saturday, waiting to see *The Bridges at Toko-Ri* at the Colonial Theater. He was friendly. We talked some. He asked where my mother had learned to play the piano so well. I got to boast—felt good even if the details were not very meaningful to him."

"That's Kenneth St. John, the baby-faced troublemaker. He was mean

when he was with a buddy. He had black spots on his teeth and claimed
he never went to the dentist. He got squashed regularly by the teacher—
Mr. Philbrook—there he is, who then had trouble being serious with him
because Kenneth always had some wiseass response which the teacher
found funny—of course, we laughed, too. I was amazed—nothing
bothered him, not even his terrible teeth. Had a DA—another juvenile
delinquent in development."

"What's a DA?"

"Short for duck's ass. A type of haircut styled after Elvis, and a sure
sign to other parents of a juvenile delinquent on his way to being a
hoodlum: long hair, combed back on the sides, then parted in the middle
in the back. If you spoke to Kenneth, his answer had an edge, like 'What'd
you speak to me for?' Rumor had it that he had a half-brother in jail."

"Lester Madden. When his mother died sometime earlier that year,
we all signed a card. It was hard for me to imagine that he no longer
had a mother. Was always being told to spit out his gum, but never
learned. Never knew anything. His farfetched answers provoked ripples
of laughter through the classroom. I thought he was cool scuffing along
in his cat boots—"

"Cat boots? What were cat boots?"

"Low, black leather boots with a D-ring on the side. They pull on and
fit loosely, so the heel drags at every step. Wear them and you were again
flirting with juvenile delinquency. When horsing around, he could make
like he pulled a switchblade out of his boot and bury it in the other guy's

Williams 1956
Seventh Grade

chest—all in one quick move. I envied his smoothness, but now I realize this smoothness was fathered by an even more important skill: being able to act without analysis. His father was the cook at Mrs. Quigley's Home Lunch—they bought a few ducks and geese from us at Thanksgiving and Christmas.

"Shawn Stackpole. When he spoke to smaller kids like me, he was always a little too loud and a little too close. Liked to show off his pictures of naked women—kept them inside his shirt. Sent to the principal a lot. Talked big about taking things and stealing from stores and never getting caught. Muscled smaller kids. If he asked me for half my popsicle, it was not a question. I only resisted when I was with friends: otherwise I resignedly broke it in half. I wasn't tough enough to resist. I remember one time when Lester came by, as he was attempting his extortion shit, and told him to get lost—boy did that feel good.

"Ken Kirkland. He sat next to me in class."

"He had a funny face."

"Yes, kind of squinchy, but amazing red hair. Lived on the Togus Road, close to the VA hospital. His father was a salesman at Farrell's—had the same amazing red hair—always said hello to me when I went in there looking at clothes. He got excused early from school several times a month—something was wrong with his mother, I think, but it was never discussed. He was one of these kids who got good grades—turned his homework in on time without any goofy excuses, seemed to have a good memory, and usually had the right answers—I liked that. But when he got a paper back or a test with a good grade, he seemed indifferent. I never understood that, but I envied his indifference."

"You couldn't fake indifference?"

"No. Just wasn't in the cards. Like Yeats saying he wanted to be a 'predatory man of action.' It was beyond his reach."

"Vince Sanders. Big belly and an old jalopy, which he raced around the field next to his house. So cool—I drove it once. His house was kind of unkempt, the lawn mostly dirt, parts of old cars lying around, and lots of children whom he called 'cousins.' See, that's so typical—"

"What's so typical?"

"I never questioned anything. I never thought maybe those kids were not cousins. Things were not too well supervised. He had my mother as a teacher in first grade at Chelsea, then they moved to Augusta. Had a collection of Nazi knives and WWII bayonets that he got from an uncle or from his father—"

"They were actually his?"

"Yes—well, anyway, he had access to them, whosever they really were. He brought some of them to school once for a report project. They were scary to handle. They smelled of death, like the slaughtering knife my father used, of death or unspeakable damage. In front of him is Louis Whitney. Pale, blond hair, flattop—that's the kind of haircut I wanted, since I was positive it would reshape my too-round face and change my life forever. And since my mother couldn't have done it—too technical—I would have to go to the barber like every other normal person. He always had nice clothes, new clothes. Fidgeted all the time; couldn't pay attention to anything. When Mr. Philbrook called on him he was often not on the right page—sometimes he didn't even have the right book open. But, he was a great dancer. He could do amazing stuff—as good as people on TV. That people were watching never seemed to bother him. His Elvis imitation was amazing. He was in Chizzle Wizzle when we were just freshman."

"That's Jeff Norton. Broke his leg skiing one winter. He was on crutches for a while, then clomped around on a cast with one crutch, then started hopping wherever he needed to go. We wrote stuff on the cast—I just signed my name, but other kids wrote clever stuff, or so it seemed to me. Laura Macintyre wrote—"

"Which one's Laura?"

"Not here. She was in the other seventh-grade class. She wrote her name in lipstick! Once for a report he brought in a Silver Star and some other medals from an older brother who was killed in Korea. Reading the citation, he started to cry. I felt bad that he had lost his brother, worse that he cried in public. The teacher had to finish it for him. In the end the teacher was crying too, but she hid it better. When I got older, I realized how minor were the tears and how enormous was the loss."

"Who's this guy? Looks kind of blank."

"Like I said, that's Richard Boucher. He looked like there was not much money at home, but making such judgments was frowned on in my house. He didn't go when we went on a class trip to the Pejepscot Paper Mill—everyone had to bring in a dollar for lunch in their cafeteria. Often wore clothes that were not in great shape or very well cared for. I tried to say hello to him. French Canadian—the words in his sentences piled up at the end. Bought a box of Cracker Jacks every day—in fact, kids called him Cracker Jacks; sometimes he gave me the prizes. In the winter he wore a short red wool jacket that said DEMOLAY on the back. I once asked him what it meant—his answer was vague—something about a secret Catholic society. I sensed that he thought telling me even that was too much. If it was so secret, how come its name was on his jacket? The obvious was always escaping me."

———

In fact the organization was named after the legendary last Grand Master of the Templars, Jacques de Molay. They arrested him on false charges. The Pope stood by while they slowly tortured him to death. The Templars were too rich and too secretive and, because of their wealth, too powerful. Catholic kings wanted their money; the Pope probably wanted them out of the way politically. I wonder how much of the story these neophytes had been told. Come to think of it, they probably blamed the Jews. Cheap shot? See Chapter 36 of A Passage to India, *where, after the trial and the recanting and the racial turmoil and trouble breaking out all over the Subcontinent and the Foreign Office posturing and the goings-on with the colonial elite, Heaslop says, "My personal opinion, it's the Jews." Spare me.*

This type of event, with its stunning savagery against their own people, was repeated in 1767, when the Jesuits were expelled from Latin America. Again, too much money, too secretive, bylaws and organizational structure that nobody could understand, and rife with "foreigners." The leaders of the lands surrounding the Jesuit areas (now in and around the modern Paraguay)—the Audiencias, *the* Captains General, *and the viceroys, wanted them out because of their political power and because they wanted the Jesuits' vast land holdings and their successful agricultural operations; the slave traders wanted them out so that they could freely raid the* reducciones de indios *that the Jesuits had set up over the centuries for the protection of the indigenous peoples.*

"This is Mr. Philbrook?"

"Yes. He coached some of the sports—maybe all of them. Maybe he taught health to the eighth-grade boys, too, health being the standard euphemism for any boys' class having to do with girls or, by using the appropriate code words, sex."

"You were in that class in eighth grade?"

"He didn't make the move to the new, consolidated, junior high—at least I don't remember seeing him. And I don't remember any such class."

"So where'd you get your sex education?"

"Nowhere. About the closest we came was my parents buying a book called *The Facts of Life and Love For Teenagers.* Must have been a bestseller: a sex-education book without any sex in it. Maybe some knee-squeezing—"

That's Richard Colfer. He stuttered, and the other kids laughed at him and mocked him. But I remember that when he was in the sixth-grade play, he didn't stutter at all. He had the most trouble during math. His father worked in the pharmacy at LaVerdiere's. My mother got prescriptions there and mentioned several times how nice he was."

"Anyone ever tell you your father was nice?"

"The kosher-style butcher in town once said he was famous—he was embarrassed—I was embarrassed. If only he had thought himself great, it would have been less embarrassing to think of him as great.

"Anyway, Richard wore his father's old Army field jacket in the winter with the insignia still sewn on. Too big for him—a lot too big. I daydreamed about belonging to the distant and exciting battalions represented by those insignia. He went down to the teachers' room once a week for speech therapy.

"Rob Bridges. He lived on Riverside Drive. He's the one I told you about who had this fantastic collection of butterflies—all pinned and labeled. His mother worked at Renee's, where we got sodas in the summer. He worked there too in the summer. I saw him once at the quarries. We were in Cub Scouts together."

"What was Cub Scouts like?"

"It was okay, I guess. I liked going to the den mother's house. And the uniforms and patches and daydreaming about moving up to more advanced levels and buying gear at Farrell's. My father certified my excellence in boxing . . . Trying to hit him produced a storm of embarrassed laughter on my part. Pretty obvious where that came from.

"Rob's father ran the feed store where we bought our grain; the cavernous warehouse smelled like alfalfa, heavy and sour. I went fishing with him and Charlie—Charlie was one of his cousins—and his father one year. It was so much fun to go zooming around Three Mile Pond in a motor boat. The fishing part was not so much fun, since you have to sit and be quiet. We only caught yellow perch, but a fish on the line, any fish, was still exciting. His father let Rob steer the boat some."

"Who's this girl—pretty, isn't she?"

"That's Nancy Cummings. Real popular. If she was alone and I walked by her, it was okay. But if she was with other girls, it was terrifying."

"And this other pretty one?"

"Patricia Stanford—they called her Pat, I think. She also came to the house for piano lessons, during which I probably developed a pressing need to straighten up the barn.

"That's Charlie Nash. He was the only other kid who already wore glasses. Had a job at Stackpole's after school—sometimes working behind the counter in the soda fountain. They made the best hot dogs there because they buttered the rolls and grilled them on both sides. His father picked him up on his way home from his job at the Post Office. If I had stayed late at school and wanted to wait around until five o'clock, I could get a ride with him to the end of our road."

"How far did that leave you?"

"I had to walk or thumb the two miles home—carrying my books.

The days before backpacks."

"You seem to remember the other students pretty well."

"Actually, I cheated a bit. I paid someone to go into the school archives and photocopy the attendance registers of the sixth and seventh grades. Once I had a name, I found I could remember a lot, but without the name—the faces in the picture were familiar, but I had lost the connection to a name. I kind of backed into it— That's Tom Carleton. When we were in the sixth grade, Mrs. Malcolm caught him and Seth playing with their jackknives during recess. She took them away and called the parents, I guess, because I saw Tom's mother come into the school during lunch, probably for some wretched conference. That was the worst—when you had to sit and listen to the teacher talk about you in the third person to your mother or father—and you're sitting right there! He was the last kid picked up on our bus, right after Janice Halloway. His parents ran the Esso station and store near Parker-Danner—"

"And Parker-Danner was?—"

"A cool place because they sold, or sold and rented, machinery and heavy equipment. Tom worked at the store weekends and summers. In the winter he used to help his father with their snow-plowing business, running the snow blower while his father plowed with their 4WD pickup truck. He said his father gave him a dollar for every driveway they did. His brother Ralph pitched for Cony; I remember seeing his picture in the *Kennebec Journal*. I think Tom was the best baseball player at Williams after Larry— That was my other good friend, Larry Jameson."

"This is the baseball player?"

"No, different Larry. Unlike the rest of us, he rarely wore sneakers— his mother worked at the Hazard Shoe Factory, and they didn't make sneakers. I once went there with him. The mill was past Fort Western, and his mother was taking us somewhere after work—Scouts maybe. The place seemed beyond comprehending. Stairs, stairs, hallways, humming, vibrating, dimly lit. I saw people punching out on the time-clock—I had never seen one before. It made that big *schlumpfff* with such authority. Then she had to explain to me that if you didn't punch your card, you didn't get paid. How, I remember wondering, how that could be? We saw her narrow working space, with the close smell of raw leather and machine oil, the sinister needle of the giant sewing machine, long and heavy—nothing like on my mother's machine at home. Shiny spinning pulleys drove multiple exposed belts; the bright lights near the work tables seemed almost too bright, yet toward the roof everything was dim. Rows of workers, right and left, rows stepping up like giant bleachers. He also had a DA, which he used to comb about ten times a day. He was the only kid in the grade who got blue suede shoes when the Elvis song hit the charts. He never spoke about his father, and once in a while he had to stay home to take care of his younger sister if she couldn't go to school. He was a nephew of one of the second-grade teachers. Always bumming stuff—from me, from Charlie, from anyone: pencils, paper, Necco Wafers, Life Savers, five cents, twenty-five cents, half a sandwich. Apparently it never occurred to him to pay it back, but that was okay because he was a friend, and boy, were friends important. Lived out on North Belfast Avenue past Bolton Hill Road—you remember, I pointed it out to you when we were going to the ag show last winter? A small house with a shed roof and dark-red asbestos siding. But, like all the other houses, it's gone now, too."

"You stayed in touch?"

"No, like all my friends, they just drifted away after seventh grade. I don't remember ever seeing Larry at Buker School. I'm not sure why that happened— Peter Peterson. Tallest kid in our grade. I remember him as tall, very blond, and dull. Slouched when he stood. Chuck used to call him a dumb Swede, sometimes to his face. Peter answered him, but his words had no venom. He was a master marble player. He talked a little funny, slightly mouthing his words. Shawn used to mimic him cruelly, making slobbering noises. I laughed with everybody else, but I knew I was not supposed to be laughing. At our house you were not allowed to make fun of others' shortcomings. He went to speech after Richard Colfer. His grandfather was an older man who helped out sometimes at Auclair's Candy across the street—I pointed it out to you on Bangor Street, now a bicycle shop—so on those days he was a great guy to go over there with. You were guaranteed special treatment."

"And this is you, of course. Great clothes styling! Who's your tailor?"

"I know, I know: awful. Fuck. My father knew style, he had once had beautiful clothes—and he still had a few of them. What was the big deal? He couldn't be bothered to make minor adjustments?"

I look at the person in the picture—I could tear my skin off with my fingernails—I ask myself, "Why is this person alive? To what end is this person living?" I waited for an answer; when I see it, even today, I'm still waiting—

"Wayne Jackson. Acted unfocused—like he was never paying attention to what you are saying. Looked away frequently when he was talking to you. Used to answer some questions OK in class—not like Louis. Kind of dark skin, low brow, thick hair. Father ran off with another woman—so Larry Jameson's mother said. His sister had to drop out of high school and go to work at the mill to earn money. He got thrown off the school bus that year for getting in a fight, but at school I never remember him getting in trouble. When he couldn't ride he was always late for school because his sister dropped him off on her way to work."

"Well, enough on that picture. What's in that other box?"

"The really old pictures: 1920s, 1930s, before they were married."

"This is your father?"

Henry, New York, 1938 © John Mills

"Yes, about the time he married my mother. That's his macho, artist's working-class outfit—and the photo is also by John Mills Sr."

"He looks like a cool guy. Where is he?"

Muriel, 1938

Mommy at piano, by John Mills Sr.

"Up on some roof, I think— And here's another picture—even older: he and a friend clowning around before a trip to Montreal— And here's a picture of my mother at her grand piano."

"She was very pretty, and kind of regal looking."

"Yes, it is easy to see why my father fell for her—at least after he decided she wasn't a lesbian."

Henry and Muriel, Yaddo.

"You gotta be kidding!"

"No. He walked into Yaddo—"

"Yaddo?"

Henry & Lester Winter Off to Toronto, 1924

"Yes, the artists' colony near the racetrack in Saratoga Springs. For those selected, you got free room and board and no responsibilities, so you could concentrate on working on whatever you wanted, or on nothing at all. It was the summer of 1938, and there she was, talking to a woman friend. One glance and my father was sure he knew everything about her he ever wanted to know. But it wasn't long before they were circling each other like a couple of wary boxers— That's the two of them at Yaddo, I think."

"Where's their wedding picture?"

"Not sure there was one. The only people who attended the rather pedestrian wedding at City Hall were my mother's parents, and for them it was not the most festive of days— That's Daddy at Norridgewock in Maine, 1932. Playing croquet."

"What was he doing there?"

"Working on *Call It Sleep*."

"Neat." She held up a photo. "This your baseball team? Who's in this group?"

"They were mostly eighth graders, so I don't remember many of them. Let's see, that's Larry Conklin, a star athlete, and from a very athletic family—a brother and a sister, that I can recall, also athletes. He very nicely spent some time with me that year, trying to get me to catch better. I was hopeless. And I think he was on the track team— That's Raymond Zackman. Very handsome. He had a girlfriend—Ellen Woodruff—we saw her in the other picture. I remember her because she was the daughter of the mechanic who fixed our car. Raymond had a killer smile. He wore khaki pants and a jacket with a turned-up collar—near the unreachable summit of 'cool.' Spoke slowly, looked directly at you. I heard girls talking about him. He was always the last on any alphabetized student list, so the teacher inverted the list sometimes to make things fairer. My parents commented on the awful color of his house—dark purple—whenever we drove by. 'Aubergine,' my mother would say. Eggplant. The timbre of her voice changed somehow. Her French was excellent. My father seemed pleased by it. I heard Mr. Philbrook call him Romeo— And I remember him—Howie Young—an eighth grader. A

Henry. Croquet. Norridgewock, Maine, 1932.

bully. I've heard him make snide, Jew-boy remarks about another kid named Larry Broder. I would look away, embarrassed— That's Chuck Hankins—also no friend, but nowhere near as bad as Howie. His father owned Hankins Hardware. He played in the junior, afterschool football league. Liked to use the word 'niggers' when addressing a bunch of us. I was embarrassed because I was told at home never to use that word. He voiced the opinion last year that 'New York Jews' were trying to ruin his father's business—this was in response to a huge Hardware Mania store opening out past Damon's on Western Avenue."

"Damon's?"

"That pizza and sub-sandwich place we went to waiting for the Subaru to get serviced? Growing up we never went there. Another place we never went to was Perry's Nut House down near Belfast."

"Why did you want to go there anyway? Just because it seemed to you that everyone else did?"

"Sure. I stopped there several years ago—nothing interesting. Sugar and souvenirs. Anyway, Hardware Mania was a chain—they already had stores in Lewiston, Portland and Bangor. He went to camp in the summer—gave a report once in class describing a typical day there. I thought it sounded like a great place."

She put the picture down. "Okay, okay, enough for one night . . . to be continued!"

David was tired of the pictures, tired of attempting to breath enough life into a jumble of images to construct one of his own. Those years, with their endless stories, their sharp turns, their ever-hopeful revisions and inexplicable contexts, slid through his mind like barbed wire through a bare hand, each barb a knot in a savage log raking him with regret for his lack of cleverness, his failure to focus, his failure to anticipate nearly everything.

Chapter XXIV

Touch Football

There was always a sense in the house—maybe like a flock deciding it was time to head south—a sense when his parents had had enough of parenting or just wanted to be alone: They moved too much, kind of milling, without immediate purpose—as if the furniture had been moved or the size of the chairs was suddenly altered. Maybe it was sex? Go! Soon! That David hadn't practiced or had his homework checked all of a sudden lost all importance. The morning had gone without incident: cleaning the duck house, pulling up the now-dead plants in the garden, raking the foolish leaves. The slaughtering for this week was finished yesterday—a relatively easy day.

The phone rang; Jerry got it. Allen. Touch football. Permission was assumed—they just got their jackets and headed out.

"Right—as usual. Permission could be assumed if Jerry wanted to do it," David thought. But if I wanted to do something in which Jerry had no interest, I would receive some of his patient, tiresome, child-management: something indicating how desperately the world needed improvement and the important role I could play if only I would modify my perverse desires.

Fall brought a few games, unpleasant but unavoidable, where neighborhood kids of widely varying sizes, ages and abilities gathered to argue, run around, and tell lies. The fields were unmarked, the stubble left after the last mowing now dry and sharp. Since the lines were largely imaginary, staying in bounds or getting a touchdown often depended on how convincingly the runner, absent any supporting evidence whatsoever, could argue his case: age, size, and popularity occasionally made the final decision indistinguishable from subornation of perjury. The game ended when the players got tired or tired of the arguments, or a score of one hundred to seven convinced the losing team that further effort was futile.

Sweaty T-shirts, stretched from being more than "touched," raucous self-promotion, scratched-up arms. The game wound down. Players drifted off—probably chores to do—maybe Sunday dinner. Jerry headed home. Those who lingered retrieved their jackets against the increasing chill of the short, fall afternoon and proceeded to offer impassioned opinions on the prospects of a favorite football team or on the coming basketball season or on how they were going to trash Gardiner High School after we beat them in the annual football game. Gardiner was Cony's archrival. As Carthage in the eyes of Porcius Cato, the town and everything in it was reflexively denounced. Intended abuses, the more improbable the better, were happily accepted by the listeners as if they had already happened. Finally, even Gardiner got stale.

"Wheah's Joe?" John Trask asked, of no one in particular.

"He's not allowed out of the house all fall, except for school and chaws," offered Butch. "Old man Jameson caught him tryin' to tip one of his cows, and told his fatha. His fatha hit him with his belt—liked to've killed him."

Cows sleep standing up. It is possible, but very difficult, to sneak up on them from behind and give them a good push. They will fall over as if made of plastic. This is not a harmless prank. The animal could break a leg or, if full, rupture the udder, either outcome making her good only for dog food.

"It isn't possible anyway," David objected. "I tried it last week with Ronny. They always wake up.

"Yeah?" countered Butch, now challenged, "What do you know, you little shit? Chahlie Buhton actually did one real good ova on South Belfast Avenue."

The fact that Charlie was nowhere around, and South Belfast Avenue was a good three miles away insulated the retort from further investigation.

"I still don't believe it," David managed weakly.

Roger Littlefield changed the subject. "I'm goin' to my uncle's huntin' cabin next weekend with my dad and my brotha." He was an eighth grader; David envied his good looks and confidence. "Deah season opens up thea this week."

"Where'z'at?" someone asked.

"Up neah Bingham. It's down this long loggin' road. Then we have to pahk the truck'n walk as fah as from heah to Steven's Road."

"What's in the cabin?" David asked.

"Bunks, a woodstove, cookin' stuff, blankets. Outhouse, but you can't get to it from inside, you hav'ta go outside. Get wata from Screech Pond." He sounded slightly annoyed, as if describing the shack was interrupting the flow of the story. "My uncle does the cookin'—we eat soooooh much!"

"You hunt?" Ray Andrews asked.

"Nah, I only got a twenty-two and my fatha won't let me use it. But next yeah foh shoa," he continued, just a little too quickly, as if to squash any further discussion of whether this actually might happen. "My fatha uses a thirty-aught-six, but my uncle," Roger said, here pausing for effect, "uses a forty-four magnum rebohd to a forty-five-seventy!"

Rifle bore sizes: .3006", .44", and .4570"—the last of sufficient power to bring down an elephant. For a deer, nonsense.

"So what do you do all day, listen to the radio?" John pressed.

"Rob and I go downwind and drive," he said, with great anticipation.

To drive is to walk through the woods making noise, pushing any deer downwind toward the waiting hunters. You will also be in the line of fire. A tale of danger survived, or one demonstrating utter disregard for safety, was only slightly less valuable than those perennial leaders: sex, liquor, and undiscovered thievery.

"My uncle gets a deah every yeah. One yeah he got two, and almost got caught by the game wahden. He was waitin' by my uncle's truck when they came out carrying just one of them. But, that's 'cause there was only three of them huntin' that day—normally his brother was theah, too, and he would have helped carry out the second." The fear of authority briefly dampened the listeners' enthusiasm. "But the best paht is, my uncle brings his magazines. We ain't supposed to look at them, but we sneak looks, like when one of them is busy with the guns or somethin', or cookin', and the other one goes to take a shit. Rod and me take turns— we don't both look at 'em at the same time. Oh, those magazines, you wouldn't believe!" His eyes lose focus, glistening.

Breathing slows, pulses quicken; invisible strings connecting the listeners to the speaker quiver, tight as piano wires.

"Thehs all these pitchas of women with big tits and theah legs spread and nothin' coverin' theah pussies, and sometimes you kin see the crack through the heah, and some of 'em are leaning over and you can see theah crack below theah ass, and, oh, theah's even one of a woman who shaved huh pussy. God, it's so ugly, like these big lips!" Disguised disgust fills his voice.

"You jerk off from them?" mocked Jim Anderson, the only other eighth grader still hanging around. "You beat your meat?" Then, mimicking the tone of a disapproving adult, scolded, "Come on now, don't lie, tell the truth, ah! you're blushing!" And now, singing, "Roger beats his meat! Roger beats his meat! An I bet you don't get anything yet, not even a drop!"

Roger, embarrassed by the taunting but pleased at the chance to escalate the dialogue and display his own flawed knowledge of sex, turns on Jim, and, despite Jim being bigger, takes a step toward him, threatening. "How about you, huh? You stickin' it in one of ya sheep? Does it feel good?"

Now it's the other's turn to protect his superior sexual knowledge and experience. And so it goes, who does, who doesn't, who has, who hasn't, finally ending in a fight where those most invested trade mock punches and little slaps. The afternoon has ended.

"It's chore time. Gotta go," David said, picking up his stuff, glad to be free of this embarrassing interchange. He didn't allow myself to believe too much of it. This scene was repeated any number of times, with other stories, with other lies. Sometimes the stories were known to be true but were said over for their shudder effect, like when Michael Pinkam caught his finger between the drive chain and the sprocket on the hay elevator. Under crushing pressure, blood spurted out of the end of his finger like red water from a very large water pistol; the machine stopped. Finally someone thought to hit the emergency stop button, and the conveyer belt sagged backwards under the weight of the climbing load, releasing his mangled hand. Or when a kid saw artificial insemination for the first time. The vet first has to clean out the rectum and lower intestine. To do this he puts on a rubber glove, a very long rubber glove, and inserts his arm into the cow, not partially but right to the armpit. An awesome sight. Then, changing gloves, he again inserts his whole arm deep into the cow and passes it a two-foot-long rod, guiding it into the uterus by feel and experience with the already inserted gloved hand. Breathless descriptions of the arm, the openings and the depth, ricocheted off the hearers' imaginations, causing some near-permanent confusion about human physiology, and others involuntary priapic twitches.

Though required to be desperately interested in all the lurid details, David's intense embarrassment over them took a lot of the fun out of it.

Sometimes the stories could be true, like John Sweet's story about "mining" the hay bales in his cousin's barn. Bales are stored layer by layer, floor-like, as high in the barn as needed. John's cousin and a friend quietly removed one bale after another from below, hiding their work by muring up the hole, so that over time the top level of this hay floor had nothing to support it but the keystone effect of the jammed-together bales. The lack of support finally reached the critical point, and one day, when the hired man walked across what appeared to be a solid deck of hay bales, he dropped into a pit of cyclopean proportions.

"Damn near scahd him to death," John said, with great satisfaction. That it could have ended in tragedy never occurred to anyone.

Hotrods, souped-up jalopies, drag racing on Bangor Street—anything about cars made good conversation. Driving while too young was better, since it required an older accomplice, a stupid, older accomplice. Roaring down the road at just under the speed of sound was the best. Alcohol consumption and abuse glittered brightly in the grown-up firmament, a galaxy of many stars: I drank, you drank, he will drink, they were drinking, yesterday, today, tomorrow, Saturday night, next week. Short but complete storylines merely awaiting names and places. Other drugs did not yet exist. Nearly hitting a moose stupidly standing in the middle of the Interstate, stealing stuff, failing to pay, playing endless pinball by shaking the machine—all could be added to your defense fund, a fund particularly useful if conversation came too close to your own person.

Unverifiable outhouse tipping stories were okay, but the event suffered from a certain lack of expansiveness, unless the owner was in it at the time and pursued the perpetrators in vain, death in his eyes. In the same vein, based on a wager of giddy proportions, was eating Jack-in-the-pulpit root, thinking it was potato.

A Jack-in-the-pulpit root, peeled, looks like a piece of potato—in fact, it's called "Indian Potato" because the Indians knew a process to make it edible. Raw, however, it is very caustic.

Then there were the stories about making explosives. No one ever made any, but many claimed they knew of someone who did. Supposedly the concoction did not require any exotic ingredients: fuel oil and fertilizer, common enough stuff around a farm. While it was a liquid, it was inert, much like dynamite. But let it dry, and it exploded on contact. Spread a little on a step, and when a foot falls on it,

Ka-Bammm!

A kid could get a lot of mileage out of a story like that. But when scoffed at by a listener, he had to back up his story by retorts, by threats, by fighting if necessary. The truth was less important than having the story believed.

Part V

Fall

August brought shorter days and cooler nights, cold even, as any camper sleeping in an uninsulated bunk will attest. Milkweed pods, succumbing to the insistent pressure of the burgeoning seeds, burst open to the fluttering delight of monarch butterflies. In the open woods we picked bunchberries, now red, and squashed them for their intense dye, or threw them at each other. Where it was a little damp you might find a fringed gentian with its vase-like base and four fringed petals folded back like the flaps on a box of Chinese takeout. The chives we so casually grabbed in the spring now sport light-purple, fig-shaped, blossoms.

As I look back on those late-August days and think—though the air was still warm, though the fields, coaxed by the sun, radiated their soft smells, though sunny afternoons were infused with a kind of indolent timelessness—and think how the summer was even at that moment inexorably slipping toward fall and another winter, a profound sense of failure envelopes them. Where was the burgeoning of garden and field? Where was Nature that could be so open-handed, so unconcerned about overproduction, so infectious in its enthusiasm, so blind to its own wastefulness?

Frost starts in the valleys and, since our brook was the lowest point on the road, the growing season often ended by Labor Day. For a night of just a few degrees below freezing, my father might try the old trick of spraying water on the plants to keep off the frost. Otherwise we picked the last of the cucumbers and zucchini and Swiss chard; the winter squash was not affected. A sea of green tomatoes ended up on top of the refrigerator in the hope that they would eventually turn red; those deemed least likely got made into pickles. The squash plants were the saddest casualties of the frost: one day enthusiastic, spreading plants, shading their fruit with broad leaves, the next a sea of blackened tents, wilted and slack. School started, touch football on unmarked fields of sharp stubble, screens came down, storm windows washed and hung, onions pulled and dried.

With the sharp early frost, the trees turned quickly. We collected the best samples, marvels of intense colors, and pinned them on the wall. But what is one, when ten thousand thousand wave to you in unison from a clump of nearby trees? Walking near a fence row at the side of a field, you might scare a partridge. They were pretty cagey, but if you got close enough, they boiled up out of the scrub, hammering the air with their powerful wings. Near scared you to death.

Wild grapes never ripen—don't even bother picking them. We helped ourselves to the apple trees growing along the road—no washing needed. The apple trees that did not grow next to the road actually belonged to someone else, but these somebodies never took advantage of their own harvest, so we occasionally helped them out—even from Mollison's lone Wolf River—

"What is a Lone Wolf River?"

"No, no, lone means there was only one of them, at least I never saw more than one. Wolf River is the name of a very large apple—two are enough to make a pie. Not really eating apples though. Northern Spy is a really good eating apple. The Wolf River was dying: half its branches were bare and useless, like the limbs of a stroke victim.

The cider mill over on Route 3 started up. The apples went through a bath, but were not subject to further inspection. Any bugs for sure drowned; no one ever heard from the worms. The apples bobbed along a spillway and ended up in very large burlap bags, which were then stacked under the press. Each bag was sandwiched in between strong, batten-like wooden panels. As the press descended, the juice started to trickle out the edges of the bags, running down into a large vat. The trickle turned to a steady flow and then to a torrent, a waterfall. The press, eventually having exhausted the apples' juice, withdrew; the pomace, destined for the pigs, was put to one side until later. The sweet smell of the apple juice and the crushed remains of the apples attracted swarms of yellow jackets. If you contributed your own apples, you got a better price. The cider however was fungible—you took from what was already pressed.

As fall wore on, the freezes at night were sharper. Heavy frost rimed the grass, smoking in the early morning sun. The land grew somber, expectant. Careful gardeners made sure to pull up all their old plants. Berry bushes were cut back and mulched to keep the roots alive. Leaves burned with a delicious aroma, the smoke heavy with particulate matter— those were still the days when smog only happened in big, ugly cities. One of my school reading books had an illustrated story about baking potatoes under the burning leaves. I thought it was a great idea, but we never tried it.

Chapter XXV

Recess

Recesses on good days were merely uncomfortable. They were a barometer of your social acceptance, your athletic prowess, and your cleverness at manufacturing things to boast about. I buttoned the top button of my shirt; I had goofy looking amblyopia; I didn't know how to clear my sinuses properly, nor had I learned how to create those viscous wads of mucous the color of mashed oysters and spit them long distances. Home and all my parents' previous lives back as far as the Holy Roman Empire were deemed an unbreachable secret, and anyway—

"But didn't *Call It Sleep* get republished so you didn't have to be so secretive?"

"Couldn't even get that right—I was gone by that time."

"Gone? Where'd you go?"

"I ran away—in a manner of speaking—and joined the Army."

"Well, that certainly got even with everybody! What'd you do in the Army?"

"I tried to get on a survey crew, in part figuring that they would travel around a lot—maybe even overseas. I dreamt about getting on a first- or second-order triangulation crew—"

"What does that crew actually do?"

"To get the absolutely most accurate distance between two points, which could be miles apart, you had to use a survey crew and extremely precise instruments and steel measuring tapes. This in the days before lasers and GPS, of course. But I couldn't qualify because of poor eyesight, so I chose heavy equipment repair. Since it was a 'manly' job, it fit right in to my primary Army-time project: developing my masculinity (suppressing my intelligence was reflexive—an ongoing project of some years already) and learning to be one of the guys. But I never got to fix anything—I was no good at it, anyway, and they spotted my typing skills and my very high scores on their standardized tests, and, after training me to fix stuff I had little interest in fixing, detoured me to offices and paperwork."

Anyway, their accomplishments were of such strange coinage that my money was suspect if not unusable, incomprehensible. Amazing private wealth, total public bankruptcy.

My parents largely dismissed what others held important. They had jettisoned or otherwise uninstalled such a large part of who they were as to be unrecognizable. Here was no continuity; they were not models, not even for themselves, but rather an unactualized, multitalented jumble, whose lives were full of careening improbabilities.

I lacked the ante for these loud games of one-upmanship. My father had seen Ty Cobb, Lou Gehrig, and Babe Ruth play baseball at Yankee Stadium. These were valuable cards. I couldn't play them because he didn't give them to me.

My parents knew so much, and had done so much, and yet what was truly important to them was tightly packed away, and, to the world, remained invisible—a long and particularly painful kind of suicide.

"My brotha just bought a new cah, and he let me drive it," this from Walter Preston. We call him 'Stone and Cooper'—

they sell fuel oil and coal—

because he carries an arsenal of pens in one of their pocket protectors.
     "Wheh'd you drive it? On the road?"
     He was disappointed at being asked. "Pahkin' lot. Behind the ahmory."
     "What'd he buy?"
     "Fowd Fahlane. Three hundrid and fohty two cubic inches! Says it'll do a hundrid 'n twenty when it gits broken in. He's gonna get lakahs,"

exhaust pipes visible along the bottom of the car doors.

     "He just got put on full time at the mill."
     "What's he do theah?"
     "Runs machinery—he calls it a horizontal millin' machine—real complicated—he showed me a pi'ture of it—they use it to make speah

pahts for their old machines, since they can't buy 'em anymaw. After five yeahs he'll be making $2.10 an hoah—probably maw by then. Plus ovahtime! Only thing he don't like is the dehty oil—it gits on his hands and won't come off."

My father had run machinery like that during the war. He even invented a unique way to cut screw threads—should have patented it. He made one-of-a-kind dies, patterns for automated machinery. He worked at very high tolerances: easy work was plus or minus .002 of an inch,

half the thickness of a sheet of copier paper,

and he had to make all the machine adjustments by hand. He developed great skill, a real achievement. I couldn't use it, as he considered it of no value. Walter's brother? He took whatever tolerances the machine gave him. I had a million answers, and I had none. Better to play with nothing.

Once a year or so Daddy would drag the heavy, wooden tool chests out of the den and heave them up onto the kitchen table. They were mysterious, part of his former life, utterly off-limits, so opening them was an immense thrill.

They were also from a time when he was competent—more than competent—an expert. Mastery was something we had never seen in him. But alas, as he spoke about them, we could sense his ambivalence.

Under the deep, upper, bin of the largest case were a number of beautifully-made drawers of various depths, with finger-joints at all the corners and fully lined with green baize. They slid in and out effortlessly, as if oiled. He would put a couple of drops of oil on his hands before handling anything—salty sweat might cause them to rust. He might show us how some of the tools were used—how to use a machinist's parallel clamp, how to sense when a micrometer was just tight enough, how one could use interpolation by reading "between the lines" on some instrument and so increase the accuracy of the measurement. He had an amazing array of tools and gadgets, many of them, he admitted, he got from pawnshops, because during the war tools simply could not be bought. Particularly fascinating were the Jo blocks.

Johannsson blocks, after their inventor.

These steel blocks were used to support work at a convenient height and be assured that the work was absolutely level, and to check the calibration of other precision tools. They were very cool. Lapped to a super degree of flatness, these heavy metal blocks exhibited wringability, the ability of two objects that are so smooth that, having been rubbed together, they can be held up, suspended one from another without benefit of magnetism. In response to a lame what-do-you-want-to-be-when-you-grow-up assignment in the seventh grade, I chose being a machinist. Daddy dismissed the goal with a growl and a hand wave.

The first rule of recess is never be by yourself. There is strength in numbers, and only more strength in greater numbers. If you want to be by yourself, stay close to one of the teachers on playground duty.

We goofed around on the heavy metal jungle-gym. Since jungle-gyms are so unimaginative, the goal is to find the most inappropriate way to use it. Put dirt or snow on the slide and try to surf down it or go headfirst. When you can't go any higher on a swing, why, get off the swing and make it go higher empty. You might be able to clean out someone's teeth.

"Joe Cheramie went ova the pole last Satiday—ova at Farington."

Oh, Jesus! not that old stupid claim. And from Jerry Baker yet. "Oh, bullshit—he did not—it can't be done—my father says it's impossible." I felt on real firm ground here because when I asked my father he had calculated the speed needed to do this, guessing at the length of the swing chain and the weight of the kid—came out to something like forty-five mph.

"Ya? Whud does he know? Was he theah?"

I was too considerate to counter with the obvious "Were you there?" so I settled for, "He knows real advanced math and he figured it out."

"Whud is he, a math teacha? My sista had Mr. Bunka at Cony and had to do all these problems with triangles 'n sizes 'n formulas. Kin he do that?"

Actually, Mr. Bunker couldn't carry my father's lunch bucket. "He doesn't do triangles anymore—he can calculate how much space there is in an egg."

"An aaegg? An aaegg? Who wants to know that shit?"

I let it drop. Jerry developed an urgent need for the bathroom.

Getting wound up by your friends is fun—radically shortening the chains. They let go of the swing—now five feet off the ground—and you whip madly around and down. Or War—swing sideways and crash into each other. Don't be afraid to use your feet to push your opponent into a pole. Or try to break the swings through mindless abuse, crashing the heavy metal seats into each other.

Other times, arms around each others' shoulders, locked in a line, we swept across the playground, scattering all before us. It was hilarious.

———

What was hilarious about it? It was a kind of death.

Since being a sweeper was better than being a sweepee, I participated when I needed to.

The object of this next game was to get the other kid to look at your hand in which the thumb and forefinger were made into an O.

"Hey, you want these tickets to the auto show?"

You looked for the tickets? You lost.

The punishment: the winner hit the loser high up on the arm, using as much force as he cared to.

It's more painful to hit high up because you hit the end of the scapula.

If, instead of looking, the other kid got a finger in the O and forced the fingers apart, he won, giving him the same right of punishment. Each punch had to be "wiped off," else the loser could retaliate. The symbolism is somewhat embarrassing, but what did we know? It was, on a conscious level, completely opaque. Boys tolerate abuse—

boys will be boys!—

within an accepted code. If you "break the code" and threaten retaliation, look or no look, you have to enforce it every day, you have to make it stick, today, tomorrow, in the boys' room, in the street. In effect, you deny the validity of the rules and remove yourself from the group, and so lose the unspoken protection membership provides.

Several times I got to be part of a baseball game. Hey, over here!— heart pounding— Oh God, the team is almost filled!— Pick me! Pick me! Never did someone fail to judge his own past performance and rush to ruin with such eager desperation. I did wretchedly. Death is nothing compared to the thought of having to replay those games, with my lousy eyes and, before I bought a new one in the seventh grade, a glove that looked like Jimmy Foxx's, with short, fat fingers and string to replace the missing webbing. I wanted to get chosen for the pickup games at lunchtime or after school—baseball, basketball, football, anything. I wanted to be good enough to get on one of the intramural teams and play Nash or Farington or Maria Clark. I wanted to be like Larry Conklin. Larry Conklin was an outstanding athlete and good looking and personable. He was a one-man cult; there were Larry

Conklin groupies. I would have been a Joyce groupie if he had ever been around.

I did better at kickball, that is until I had the bad luck to kick the ball high and nearly foul into a crosswind, which blew the ball not into the cyclone fence, not over the cyclone fence, but on the cyclone fence. The game was over, called on account of instant deflation. However, a deflated ball is a nifty way to model the headpiece found on an electric chair.

"I bet I can hit you softer than you can hit me!"

"Okay, I bet!"

After several turns the exchanged blows are reduced to mere touches. Then the bettor slugs the other and crows, "You win!" Yuck. Anything to be agreeable. The trick is to force the challenger to go first; I never figured that out.

But a better trick is to never need to figure that out. I was never strong enough to play, or strong enough not to play. I hung on between the two worlds, desperate to belong—in ampulla pendere . . .

A new grammar school opened up the hill—up Gedney Street— named for the Hussey family, one of whose members owned the largest hardware store in town. What, if any, other civic virtues the family had displayed or continued to display were never discussed. We could take advantage of the hot lunch program by walking several short blocks. Why do all lunch rooms smell the same? Maybe it's something in the water.

No, I think it's the "American Chop Suey" an unfortunately-named, unsavory-sounding combination of ground beef, tomato sauce, cheese and elbow macaroni.

It was good, but it was safer to denounce it. "How can you eat that? I'll never be starving enough to eat that!" Part of what he said was true: he would never be starving.

"That stuff looks like a cow's afterbirth!"

I thought their fussiness remarkable. How could they refuse to eat something? Such a lack of character! At my house, the liver got finished, otherwise no dessert. I thought the food fine, but I usually kept such sentiments to myself, even when another kid gave me some part of his intolerably-prepared meal.

Before the hot-lunch program at Hussey we brought our lunches and ate them in the lunchroom, a large, rather dull place in the basement of

Williams School, with a low ceiling and a cement floor. It smelled of yesterdays' lunches, disinfectant, floor cleaner, and sour milk. Along one end, behind a wide, stainless-steel counter, was a snack bar, and along the other, a few large, low windows looking out at the playground. You could sit almost anywhere and be certain that a roof support would block part of your view. When open, the snack bar bustled with volunteers handing out milk or selling Dreamsicles, its bright lights flooding out into the room. When not, that end was dark, its stainless-steel gates forbidding and slightly repellent. In Procrustean fashion, everything happened here: Scouts, PTA meetings, movies, school assemblies, clubs, atom bomb drills. On nice days we grabbed our free milk and went outside to eat—always plenty of room to sit on the ground. A small embankment fronted on Bangor Street, the main road on the west side of the school. From there we loudly hailed the "good" cars, and assailed the "bad" ones. As there were Ford families and Chevrolet families, so were there Ford cheerers and Chevrolet cheerers. Detroit was in its neo-Gothic, living-room, period. Absent any poorly-directed interest in design or engineering, anything large and new was assured of some support. Everyone cheered the pre-WWII cars; a 1938 Desoto brought down the house. There were no Nash Rambler cheerers. A person could be marked for life by supporting the wrong car maker.

Chapter XXVI

Red Rover

A cross the street at Auclair's, a penny was all you needed for a piece of candy. Got five cents? Get one of those wax figures filled with syrup, nibble a hole in the wax, and suck out the garishly-colored sugar water. Or chew the seal off a fat Pixie Straw, and let the tart crystals—like Kool-Aid right from the envelope—dissolve on your tongue. To show off to friends, stick out your purple tongue. Or you could get a whole fistful of Bacon,

pink-and-black striped candy,

and be a big shot at recess.

None of these things were particularly good, but it was always good to have them.

With ten cents, go down Bangor Street to Barry's for an Orange Crush, the bottle mysterious, with its concentric ridges and its darkly-opaque glass. Or a Pine Cone, appropriately shaped vanilla ice cream dipped in chocolate, eaten off a stick. If you found a pink end on your stick you got a free one. If you had big money—twenty-five cents—a Table Talk pie was the best.

A five-inch pie with leathery crusts and a filling closely resembling some fruit.

At home, "spendthrift" hovered over these kinds of purchases, a term guaranteed to take any fun out of them. I learned never to say anything: only the dentist knew.

"Red Rover!"

"Where?"

"Near Doc's." The news of a game in formation spread through the groups of older boys.

Haggling starts over who should be the captains even before everyone interested has assembled. The biggest and strongest kids are suggested, the enthusiasm for each candidate carefully if informally gauged. Successive voice votes narrow the field, finally solidifying behind Howie and Chuck. The flip for first pick goes to Howie—

Howie has few friends—in this crowd I see only Kenneth St. John. Those here who can tolerate him pretend indifference, but casually shift position in order to be visible. He only came to Williams last year. He won't pick me unless forced to—he taunts me about not making the baseball team. Howie always has money—the braver kids sneeringly suggest it is not his.

He looks over the candidates and picks Dick. Chuck counters by picking John and Robert. Howie then picks Ron and Vince—and so, back and forth until there are eleven kids on each team—and that's how I ended up on Howie's team. I ditch my glasses in my jacket, and then my jacket. We line up about twenty feet apart. The captains noisily set their lines: normal strategy is to put a weaker kid in between stronger kids. I'm between Howie and Dick. The weaker guys will never try us; the big kids will wait until the end of the game when they no longer care—when it's no longer trying to get through the line, it's how abusive can you be. We picked first, they call first. Captains call—you can't Red Rover a captain unless he's the only one left. My stomach starts to tighten. We link arms, some protesting by mimicking effeminate gestures—I laugh, but the protests embarrass me—twelve- and thirteen-year-olds are terrified of touching another male. Linking arms makes for a much rougher game than holding hands. It is harder to get through—you have to commit your whole body, and, for a defender, it is much more painful when someone does get through. Chuck starts:

"Red Rover, Red Rover, send Ken right over."

The teams roar—

I roar some—

like clashing armies, howling, in a crescendo towards impact. The line sags back. Failed! Lester and Peter hold on. Cheers, the whole team cheers, it is so great!

It's not great. There's nothing great about it.

Back and forth we go, more howling, more cheers, more failures; we are playing a painful, zero-sum game, trading players.

Jeff Norton is captured by Rob and Tom, is called right back and is captured by Shawn and Charlie. Jeff is pilloried for failing to get through. Cries of "Ya didn't try! . . . ya couldn't get by Charlie, ya dink? . . . fix! fix! . . . do it ovah! . . . my sista could get through theah!" fill the air. The capturing team answers with a variety of insults centering around the woefully inadequate masculinity of everyone on the other team.

Chuck calls Vince—that was a mistake. He makes up in weight what he lacks in speed, getting between Richard Boucher and Tom. First blood. He takes John back;

if you break through, you bring another player back to your team.

Lester forearms Charlie and gets through, but on the way by, he either stumbled or was tripped by Shawn or maybe it was simply his momentum. Anyway, he ends up falling on his hands in the dirt. Lester whirls on Shawn, menacing. "You tripped me, you bastid."

Shawn colors, hesitating, but gets an immediate chorus of support from the rest of our team; they never saw what happened, but reflexively defend their own. "No, you're the bastid—you tripped on yaw own goddamned feet caus'iv how you ran into ouah line—sideways!"

Charlie is hurt and walks away, finished with the game—that's enough damage to break the standoff and avoid a fight. First casualty. Lester trots back, taking John with him. I can't see whether he's smirking. Things are starting to get ugly. A few turns later, Robert goes for Lester and Wayne; this is not the weakest link, but getting through Lester will be the best revenge. Robert manages to stay on his feet and takes back Ken Kirkland.

Here comes Wayne . . . here he comes . . . is he coming toward me? Oh, Jesus, he's coming for me! Oh, God, hold on! hold on! Howie and John tense before the immanent collision, their arms feel like steel, my arms locked between their arms and bodies. He's going between Howie and me! Oh, God!—

Wham!

The impact, the hardness, the heat of the hurtling body; the anticipation is worse than the pain, except he had his elbow out. For an instant I just swung between the other two. We captured him. I grin, red-faced but relieved. Since he didn't get through, I forgive him for elbowing me. Tears form in my eyes from the pain. I look around to see if anyone is watching, but without my glasses things are rather fuzzy.

"Way to go, David!" Howie says. Does he mean it? Is he serious? I'll take it—I blush from the unaccustomed praise, and in public no less. Howie's really not so bad, after all.

He's just below John Milton. Actually, I don't know much about John Milton, but I know he was great.

I have lost a button on my shirt—oh, well. Our line is getting longer.

Dick is called again and goes for Peter. Peter raises a leg to try to deflect the painfully anticipated assault, but Dick gets through, in spite of Chuck's strength and Peter's leg. Dick's pants get dirty, for which he snarls at Peter for playing dirty. Dick's tough, tough and big, and Peter really took a shot. He quits. The game is like tackle football without the equipment; the smaller guys are the weak links, and become targets. On their next turn, in retaliation for Peter, Richard Boucher and Tom let Ken Kirkland fly through unobstructed; his momentum puts him on the ground. Ken acts like it's nothing; it was a dangerous precedent.

"Red Rover, Red Rover, send Rob right over."

John and I capture him. Wow! Two captures in one game. My shoulder hurts up high, by the joint.

When am I going to toughen up like the other guys?

The other team is losing; things start to fall apart. Howie calls Dick "cowshit"; he charges between Shawn and Robert. In the collision, Shawn sits down hard in the dirt.

"Cowshit," Shawn mocks, "look what ya' made me do!"

"Ya staht in with me, yu'll end up smellin' like a different kind of shit!" Guffaws all around.

Jeff Norton has been called a lot; he's no longer trying very hard; Ken and Richard capture him. Robert gets called—not really trying either. The guys on our team dump on him because of his birthmark, chanting "Rooster, Rooster!"

Lester gets called. He's coming toward me! He's coming for me! Oh, shit! The guy can be a real prick— He tries to slam into me using his shoulder, but turns a little too much. His sweaty, sour, shoulder blade hits me in the face. The impact forcefully empties my lungs. He comes down on my instep—goddamn those cat boots. But the line held, we didn't let him through. That's three times today! Howie comes to my rescue:

"Ya nevah try someone big, do ya? Ya scahd? Ya goddamn right! Whyn't ya try me sometime?"

Larry snarls, insult for insult.

"Ah, why don't ya go do yah homewohk," Howie responds. Big laughs, big laughs all around.

The words sound good, but they are not mine; tears form in my eyes again. I'm always crying. Sweaty, bruised, rumpled, and missing two buttons, I pick up my jacket and fish out my glasses; the physical world gets a lot clearer. I'm quitting. The other team continues to erode.

Finally, even Dick gets captured.

"Red Rover, Red Rover, s-s-se-send R-Richard right o-oh-oh-over," Howie mimics his stutter.

Richard tries to say "You fuck" to him, but it never comes out. He gives up struggling. Everyone laughs. I laugh more quietly than the others. It's cruel. He lunges; he fails.

It is now sixteen to three for our team. Robert gets called. Instead of one, all three of the remaining players charge at Richard Boucher, going for both sides, screaming "Cracker Jacks, Cracker Jacks!" He lets them through, and the three run off the field, screaming the same epithet at the top of their lungs. The final laugh. The game breaks up—everyone has had enough. I go to look for Charlie, I can't find him—maybe he went in. I see Howie and Kenneth heading to the store—I want to avoid them—his previous praise signifies nothing; he's still the same son-of-a-bitch, and if he is not clever enough to be mean, why Kenneth tutors him.

Howie stole one of my spiral-bound notebooks, and when I accused him of it, we got in a fight. He tore my shirt. Where were my parents? Why did my father never defend me?

I turn and go around the building the other way, around the back door.

Walking, a record starts to play, my record, slow . . . slower . . . alone . . . I always . . . the voice deepens, the words distort . . . Red Rover, Red Rover . . . I was neither strong enough to enjoy the game, nor confident enough to dismiss it . . . Red Rover, Red Rover . . . The game was important, the game was not at all important . . . Red Rover, Red Rover, send someone right over. I was waiting for myself, for a sense of mastery, a sense of ownership . . . Red Rover, Red Rover . . . it never came over . . . Red Rov . . .

I see Betty Saunders, and walk over. She is waiting for her turn at hopscotch. Hopscotch is such a quick and easy game; all you need is a stick, a rock, and a level patch of dirt. Boys seem to outgrow it earlier than girls, and then they only play when they are goofing around.

"You seen Charlie?" She is another cousin of Charlie's.

"He went inside; said he'll be back soon."

Joan Riordan gets through 4's. I'm about to continue walking, when Charlie comes out with a popsicle.

"How are you?"

He looks sad. "That son-of-a-bitch really meant to huht me. Wait'll he comes into the stoah with—who's that gurl he likes to hang around with—the one with the big tits and the sleeveless blouses?"

Some days you can even see part of the white cup.

"Oh, Stella?" I try to sound casual.

"Yeah, that's huh, anotha dumb Canuck. Good enough faw him. Wait'll they come in. I'm gonna' pick my nose and put it in his milkshake!" Then abruptly changing the subject, "You want half? It's grape."

"No thanks—don't like grape."

While we are discussing further retribution, some of the girls abandoned the hopscotch game in favor of jumping rope with Maggie McGuire. Janice Halloway was already on sixes. I jump in after her, singing: "With CAT-like TREAD, upON our prey we STEAL, NO sound at ALL, we NEVER speak a WORD, a FLEA'S foot FALL would be diSTINCTly heard. Taran-tarah!"

Charlie looks at me with a sort of good-natured pity. "Is that supposed to be funny? Tell me when to laugh. Wheah do you get such stupid shit?"

"It's Gilbert and Sullivan. I saw it this summer down near Brunswick."

"Is that 'Sullivan' Ed Sullivan?"

Now it's my turn to pity. "No, it's not that Sullivan. This Sullivan lived in 1890—in England." Blank. Mars is only slightly further away than 1890's England. But unlike some others, he lets it drop.

Towards the Quimby Street gate, cheerleaders and wannabes start cataloging the hierarchy of the basketball team for the umpteenth time. "Walter Evans is our man, if he can't do it . . ." The cheerleader falls to one knee, and passes the baton of adoration to the next girl who immediately adds, "Jim can. Jim Gordon is our man, if he can't do it . . ."

We clunk through our game, sometimes keeping time with the cheerleaders, sometimes substituting silly names. If we step out, we just continue. Scoring is not an issue. From the cheerleaders, the Ouija ball of hero-worship floats briefly in the air—the next name floats to the top:

"John McFarlane is our man, if he can't do it . . ."

"Larry can." Oh sure, he always gets named last. Then altogether, on tiptoes, nearly bursting: "Larry Conklin is our man. If he can't do it, NO ONE CAN!" Yuck.

The cheerleading crew went across the street to get sodas. Actually Nancy Cummings decided to go and the rest followed, secretly hoping to divert the attention of one of her admirers, or in any event, for sure to scavenge from her rejects. She is very popular; the guys lower their voices when they talk about her. She won't even say hello to me. Probably just as well; I haven't a clue what I might say in return.

I saw her and her friends at Mike's Lunch last week. I don't usually go there because it's a high school hangout, but I was with my brother. A couple of tables over were Donny Roberts and Brian Sweet—both freshmen. The cheerleaders came in, confident, ambling, clustered. Nancy asked Donny if they could sit at his table. He appeared unimpressed and said, "No." Just like that, right to her face. "No." How could he? When Nancy Cummings is expecting a yes answer, no becomes a logical impossibility. Her friends tightened at his abruptness, but Nancy, rolling her hips slightly, gave him a condescending smile that said, "Who cares?" He became invisible. Her friends watch to see how it's done. Tonight, while supposedly doing their homework, they will practice in front of a mirror. When she had picked a table, Donny, if he cared to look, saw only her back.

* * *

"You caddying this summer?"

"Ya—definitely. I got out of goin' to that stupid camp faw a month, so I got the whole summa. Except faw my fatha's vacation—weah goin' to Nova Scotia. Weah gonna take the ferry from Pohtland one way—ya know—the Bluenose Ferry, that takes yaw cah too. You goin' to that music camp?"

"For a month. Otherwise going to hay, I guess."

"What'ya do theah? Is it like a regula camp, or d'ya have to play some instrument all day? Oh, maybe you sing that Gilbaht stuff!"

"No Gilbert stuff. Not sure how it goes. I think we take lessons and rehearse in the morning. Rest after lunch, then swimming skills and waterfront and stuff like softball or tennis, or if you want, you can practice on your own."

"Have you seen it?"

"No. We got their catalog."

Maggie has lost her jump-rope players—all but Kathy deserted in favor of a dodge-ball game informally supervised by Mrs. Cline. Maggie approaches us. "You wanna swing the rope for us? Everyone else left." She turns her body slightly to one side and puts her hand behind her far hip, tightening her blouse. She lowers her chin with a smile, and waves the rope in my direction. I like the smile; I missed the rest of her message. And she asked me, even though she's in Charlie's class. I glance over at Charlie; he shrugs.

"Okay," I tell her. "What are you going to do?"

"'Miss Suzy,' then 'Peppa.'"

"It's too long," objects Kathy. "Let's do 'Down in the Valley.'"

In the middle of the argument, Helen comes over.

She is so pretty. She is Kathy's friend, and needs no invitation—she is certain of acceptance. She never feels it necessary to calculate likelihoods.

"I want to do 'Miss Suzy,'" Maggie says, as if she's stamping her foot without moving it.

I don't like the arguing, because in a second I'm going to get asked to take sides with one or the other, and it's just so hard to disagree with a girl, any girl, for sure with a pretty girl like Helen and when you say something they don't like their face kind of hardens and that's the end of the smiles until they need something else which they act like will be never. Maggie gets her way.

Maggie owns the rope, and directs traffic. "Helen, you staht."

We swing. The ball gets loose from Mrs. Cline's game and rolls toward me; I push it away with the outside of my foot. Helen jumps in, skipping, the song heavily syncopated:

> Miss Súzy had a báby, his náme was Tiny Tím,
> She pút him in the báthtub, to sée if he could swím.
> He dránk up all the wáta and áte up all the sóap,
> He tríed to eat the báthtub, but it woúldn't fit down his thróat.
> Miss Súzy called the dócta, the dócta called the núhse,
> The núhse called the lády with the álligata púhse . . .

When the song finally finishes we go immediately to "Peppa,"

turning the rope as fast as we can.

She gets to fifteen.

Joan, evidently disenchanted with dodge-ball, disengages; she drifts back in our direction. Kathy goes next. Misses just before we go to "Pepper." She's out. Maggie gets ready; the rope turns; instead of jumping in, she hesitates. "You guys ah tuhning too fast!"

Helen objects immediately. "They ah not; theah tuhning it just like they did faw me; you just wanna win!"

Maggie insists again that we are in fact turning too fast. Annoyed, she senses Joan watching, expectantly. She turns on her. "You can't skip heah any maw 'cause ya left!"

The girls glare at each other for a second. Stung, Joan turns abruptly; walking away, she raises her voice and flings over her shoulder, "You cheat anyways."

Maggie jumps in, fast or no. The bell rings while she is in "Pepper," and it distracts her enough to miss at thirteen, a failure she immediately blames on our ineptitude or deliberateness. Oh God! She's sulking. We get no thanks.

Recess is over.

Chapter XXVII

Belonging

Hugh and Jeremy, 2006

I belonged nowhere. It has taken a lifetime to shake loose of what seems a well-meaning conspiracy started by my parents, which effloresced into a cankered vine with great, if never-realized, potential. It is an old story, tiresome, self-involved, and so, easily skipped or trivialized. I was supposed to have been a girl and a talented musician (better, a very talented musician); I instead had the temerity and poor judgment to be a boy who wanted to be just exactly like his father. Whatever he knew, I wanted to know. Whatever he had done, I wanted to do. My mother did not approve.

"How did you know she didn't approve?"

"She would occasionally give me, *sotto-voce*, helpful advice like: 'Don't be like your father!' or 'Never have liver and onions at the dinner celebrating your wedding.'"

"Not eating liver sounds like good advice—at any time."

"You're thinking of a slab of meat the color of Oklahoma after a dust storm, overcooked, and roughly the shape of Ireland seen from deep space. But livers from our geese, broiled, mashed, with a little schmaltz, served on toast with salt and pepper—"

"Why do you have to keep using these Jewish words like 'schmaltz'?"

"You're just miffed because so many of them have become part of English, and they are so delicious to say. What'd you guys contribute? 'basket'? What an interesting word!"

Somewhat to the right of not belonging was the desire to be invisible, a desire often associated with farm-related chores like picking up the lettuce scraps from the back of local supermarkets or carting barrels of waterfowl guts to the Augusta Tallow Company or with going shopping with my father's New York relatives, Jewish, overweight, with funny accents and city expectations, or with the lack of basic amenities like running water or with opera on the radio on Saturday afternoon or the urea-sharp smell of boiling kidneys for the dog or with my father launching into a short performance from *Finnegan's Wake* when there were friends around or with the lack of anything looking like soda or potato chips in the house.

One of the biggest favors I could do my parents was not getting sick, since that might require parental involvement and a trip to the doctor. Allergies were not allowed. If you fell while learning how to ride a bike, you should learn in such a way that this would not happen. (It would actually be better if you knew how to ride without having to learn.) If you went into the ditch and split open your scalp by hitting your head on the end of the culvert, why, here's a cold facecloth. The other equally powerful reason not to get sick, at least early on, was that you might have to visit Dr. Daddy, who had a collection of syringes and other instruments of torture on long-term loan from the Augusta State Hospital. A shot of penicillin, whether or not medically appropriate, always cured you. Headaches were a sign of lack of character and were probably caused by spending too much time indoors or engaging in frivolous pursuits. I got even by having rotten teeth.

My parents had a number of visits from the FBI, clean-shaven agents standing on the porch shouting at them as to whether they were "trying to overthrow the government by force." My father, at one point, shouted back, telling them to get off his property, and that if they had actually done anything wrong, arrest them! They interviewed our neighbors, although which of them, except Ernest, I have never learned. They came out to the haying operation once but had difficulty interviewing Ernest, as we were standing right there. Nothing good ever came from my father's communism, commitment to which, by Stalin's trial of the Jewish doctors, had eroded to the point of capitulation. Although capitalism never became the favored organization for a good society, it became clear to him that a communist revolution in America would never happen.

To further erode any hope I might have of being a normal part of society, strange people came to the house. One was a man we called "Uncle Bert"; he was a communist trying to lay low, whose real name was Mike, a man Daddy had met in Rockland several years previously. That he was at our house was obviously to be kept a secret. He lived in the "new room," painted tolerably in oil, and made good Italian food. He bought my brother and me our first skis, twelve-dollar wooden gems from Sears with cross-country bindings. Then he went away.

Another character, local but more scary, was Perley Cunningham, a nephew of sorts of Ernest. Perley had been in Hawaii on December 7th, 1941, and had island-hopped all the way across the Pacific, receiving nothing more serious than scratches and bruises. He was the middle-weight champion of the Marine Corps. He came home, got a job on a construction project, and was hit on the head by a falling tool. Maimed for life, he exhibited some of the same losses of function as a stroke victim. When sober he spoke loudly, his voice thick, his words slurred; when drunk, his voice got louder and his verbal skills fell, although never far enough to keep him from excoriating his native land and blessing the communists, who were finally going to get things right. He came by at various times, usually at night, and called my father out of bed. Occasionally Daddy got in the car and took him home. Later he started getting delusional and aggressive, accusing my father of being an informer. Between his political views and his drinking, fights were never far apart.

"So how many people came to visit you way out there?"

"Very few, and most of those came during the summer. The Farrells, once or twice a year, and once or twice a year we went up there. I'm not sure what we did about seating—the kitchen table did not seat eight people—if the weather was good we could eat on the porch. My parents were pretty alone."

"Maybe the table had leaves?"

"No, no leaves. Once my mother invited the teachers to an end-of-school get-together. All these visits left me mortified beyond belief. I would have gladly hidden in the barn. I wanted to die.

Remembering these feelings makes me want to cut into my guts—but the mess might be an inconvenience to others.

"What were you so mortified by?"

"My life. Our lives. The universe. The wreck of a house. The ducks. The lack of running water. The immediacy of the bathroom. My father's awkwardness: he didn't really like to have people around. My mother's discomfort, unarticulated."

"Didn't you like any of the people who came to visit?"

"I was always excited when my cousins were coming—until they came. Then the discomfort started. We were close in age, and our parents liked each other—in fact they had lived together after my parents got married. Their arrival always meant that we could chuck the haying for a day and go down to the shore. The ocean might as well have been in Nova Scotia for all we saw of it in the course of a normal summer. We never went there on our own. It was a company thing, and my father never went there at all. We ran in and out of the cold breakers, explored the rocks and tidal pools, then had a barbecue."

"And your father's family?"

"When the Jews came, they were too many, too fat, too noisy, and this only intensified my father's discomfort. The non-Jews were easier for him to deal with."

"And they all stayed at your house. How did you put them up?"

"We didn't—except for my father's mother. Others we usually put up at Getchell's Riverside Motel. Guest rooms in our house were in short

Kent, Grace Parker, Betty, Wesby, Muriel, Oregon, 2013

supply, showers more so, the water rationed, and the limited bathroom facilities strained."

"What was your grandmother like?"

"By the time I knew her in Maine she suffered from dementia—my father said that her monster of a husband finally drove her into madness. She was diabetic; my father gave her shots, and sterilized the syringes by boiling them on the stove. The Jews were the most mortifying to have around, but arrived with the best food. Whooeee! A whole pastrami covered with black peppercorns, a gallon of herring in cream sauce, boxes of store-bought cake, and a loaf of rye bread two feet long! The food almost compensated for their peculiar way of speaking, their peculiar looks, their awkward bodies."

"Did you take them to the shore?"

"I don't think so—well, not to the beach. I think we took them to Pemaquid, to the lobster pound."

The summer of my eighth grade we drove to the Parker family vacation home in Monument Beach, Cape Cod. They were going to sell it—this was, then, the last get-together."

"Who went?"

"Just the three of us. My father stayed home—ostensibly because of the farm. But ten years before, this had been the site of his 'final break' with my mother's family. Her father made some tactless remark about 'keeping the Kikes out of Kiwanis.' When he objected, they told Daddy to leave. What they did not expect, though, was that my mother would leave, also."

"Who was there when you went?"

"An uncle and his wife and several of their children. And Grace Parker, my mother's mother; her father had died over ten years before."

She was a fuck, was Grace, and a sanctimonious one at that. Before they were married, my mother had asked her father for money so she could live in New York through the fall and winter and compose (she was on sabbatical). He, though a bit scandalized by her commitment to her women friends and her penchant for married men, had agreed. Then her mother got involved. The upshot was that, despite her three degrees and the year with Nadia Boulanger, and a number of years of teaching music at Western College, they decided she should go to Yale for a year and learn more about music! And no $$. My father viewed the recommendation as patently self-serving— trying to pry her away from him under the guise of sound advice.

Grace later reduced the $100 her husband had been sending my mother by $25 *because she found out that, through frugality and skimping, she had put that much into a bank account.*

"Have a good time?"

"Well, I had a time. First time away from home. Went out in their small motorboat. I remember the Manhattans that were a sort of family joke, and a crown rib roast the likes of which I had never seen."

"How'd you get there?"

"Drove in the old green Suburban—a bit embarrassing."

"Why were they selling it. Nobody around to use it?"

"Seems they didn't like the way the neighborhood was changing— too early for Blacks—probably Jews and Catholics polluting the ocean by living near it. Remember, they were real blue-bloods, one a DAR, the other, would you believe, a son of the Mayflower. That the mythical values of their fearless forebears might have been a bit vitiated over sixteen generations (or however many it had been) never seemed to bother them."

Christmas was never a big holiday—I mean the gift part. My mother cared little for it, though she was indignant over it's crass commercialism and outspoken about the spiritual mendacity of those who thus celebrated it; my father was big on not spending money. In the earlier years we got a few presents, some practical, some unexpected. There was a big Christmas when I got a pink-and-black plaid flannel shirt—I had wanted a pink one, but the giver, as a long-time friend of my mother's, might have been unable to find one in my size, or maybe decided, from good sense and sensitivity, that a nine-year-old boy should not wear a pink shirt. The second item was a cap pistol and holster, a black holster, with a thong to tie around the leg and fake bullets marching with serried regularity around the back, the wide belt itself bedizened with fake silver and even faker gems. Now I could play cowboys and Indians or cops and robbers with an enhanced sense of authenticity—or maybe it was effectiveness.

But I lived a life of being watched, of my self never really being mine, so neither the goodness of the cops nor the wickedness of the robbers could be savored: the conflict a tasteless, moral alloy. A life of Miss Pross attempting to resist a mental Madame Defarge. Knitting, knitting . . .

Then the holiday stopped, and stopped annoying my mother, and became part of her private, un-accessed past. In later years I used my haying money to buy them presents: a really good clasp knife, a badger-hair shaving brush, a beautiful two-piece dress. I have the knife. I have pictures of her in the dress. It was her dress-up dress.

At Williams School we stood as individual classes in the hall on the last day before Christmas vacation and took turns singing Christmas carols. I thought the songs were nice and participated half-heartedly—

What was I supposed to feel?

I thought the Jesus business rather overdone, but I envied the other kids, whose world, into which they apparently fit so comfortably, seemed transparently obvious. From the terrible truths at home, their world offered only awkward, transient, escapes—theirs a shallow if unreachable existence, its only solace was that I would never have it.

Religion at school was tolerated in a nondenominational way. Participation was pleasant, if mechanical. Every morning we said the 23rd Psalm, or the Lord's Prayer. Good citizenship was encouraged by hagiography and the singing of stirring songs. Vince Sanders sat near me in fifth grade. When we stood up to sing *My Country 'Tis of Thee* or the *Star Spangled Banner*, he substituted the most outrageous words— "My country's tired of me, I'm going to Germany . . ." —just loud enough to cause those around him to break out laughing, and thereby gain the teacher's attention. I was a bit silly, having suffered the dubious achievement of getting "Silly" in deportment on my report card, and so

Front Porch. Augusta, 1951

laughed louder, thereby gaining a greater share of the teacher's attention. She never heard him, or she made like she didn't.

The local kosher-style butcher shop gave my father a store calendar, which he duly put up. I would have much preferred one with pictures of the Grand Canyon. But in fairness, it was the source of my Jewish education.

"What was on the calendar?"

"I saw the word 'Purim' on one of the days, so I asked my father what it meant."

"He told me it was a holiday to commemorate the escape of the Jews from their first Hitler. But he was uncomfortable with having to tell me."

"How do you mean?"

"His tone of voice conveyed closure, like 'no more questions on that subject.' And the way he tightened his shoulders: you know how a person holds their body funny when they are uncomfortable with something or some situation? Like if you have to explain to a nine-year-old girl what that big, swinging sack is that's chafing the ankles of a big ram. If you explain it, you explain it in a voice that invites no further discussion."

My parents didn't suffer no truck with popular culture. Except for breathing, I think we were out of sync with the entire state. We didn't have a TV. *Life Magazine* was summarily dismissed, the *Daily Kennebec Journal* battered mercilessly for its lack of national news and information of substance, and if you couldn't find classical music, don't even bother to turn on the radio. I was desperate for the current idioms of youth. Repeated wheedling about watching TV and listening to popular music slowly weakened their resistance, though resignation clouded their every permission. Every hour spent in such frivolous pursuits diminished the possibility that I might become Superman, or even a competent adult. I frittered away my time in this world, and probably my share in the world-to-come. Maybe there was a mix-up at the hospital?

My main TV source was a classmate who lived a mile away.

"Oh, come on, don't bullshit me. A mile! Next time you tell me it will be two miles . . ."

"Yeah, it was a mile. Once or twice a week I would get permission to go there. We'd watch *Riverboat* with a guy named Yancy Derringer—cool name, huh?—or *Rawhide*, or *The Rifleman* with Chuck Connors. I liked the clarity of these kinds of shows and the confidence of the men:

they always beat the cruel and unredeemed."

"Nice house, I mean a bathroom and stuff?"

"I was taught never to judge, and often did not allow myself to see things. The house had a stark, brittle, quality about it, and it was only years later that I realized that in that house there was not a book, not a magazine, maybe not even a picture on the wall."

"So how did you get back?"

"Walked. Once in a while I thumbed a ride, but usually I walked."

On a clear, ten-degree night, a billion stars wheeled overhead. Except for the moon and the occasional light from a house, darkness held over everything. The pale light turned the impenetrable thickets at the side of the road into frightening possibilities: every loud noise off in the woods grew predatory eyes. On a cloudy night I often stumbled—the road dark as water, communicating nothing. A halo over the next hill signaled an approaching car, burgeoning, brightening. The power lines caught fire an instant before the headlights boomed into view, stabbing, bouncing, dying back, light gone, sound gone, silence. I felt abandoned and alone, like having a stranger leave the house after a brief visit without ever asking my name.

"And what did you do for music? Only that classical stuff? Or as your friend called it, 'Gilbert and Ed Sullivan?'"

"Once a week I got permission to listen to a popular music show called *Cream of the Crop*. For one hour. The show was actually two hours, but my parents were afraid I might become ill. To show his utter disdain for rock and roll, my father called it 'Cream of the Crap.'"

"That's funny. 'Cream of the Crap.' Was he always so funny?"

"Yeah, he was funny. He could make my mother laugh, and she didn't have too much to laugh about. He had a wonderful sense of timing. And he liked puns. Jeb got in on the act. I of course was too slow, but thought everything hilarious: 'What matter Horn what mountain we climb?' I remember was one of his. Oh, and then because my father ate so fast, he invented this cross-language phrase which he would deliver at his most fatuous: 'Parce-Porque?' punning first on the Latin word for pig, then of course Spanish."

I could only listen using an old radio at low volume in my bedroom with the door closed. We didn't heat the upstairs, remember, so in the winter I had to use a couple of wool blankets to help get me through the program—the latest hot songs just weren't hot enough. I mooned about finding love, anguished over losing love, daydreamed of having love. The cream cheese pathos of the songs kindled thoughts of everlasting happiness with some girl who was particularly fortunate for never having found out.

Movies were a big treat, a big, infrequent treat. Beside the trip into town to take us, and a second trip into town to pick us up, my father bridled at the then outrageous prices: he never failed to mention that when he was a kid, it was two for five cents, then undoing some of the good memories by confessing that he was often the sucker with the three cents.

My mother, rather too patiently, did without much during all the years in Maine. Her first teaching job in the Augusta area was in Chelsea, a neighboring town, in the one-room schoolhouse on Mud Mills Road: $1,600 per year. Until the Amana freezer came, my mother canned every year: pickles, jam, vegetables; one year she even canned meat, but I think it spoiled. Several years we had eggs in a large crock in the cellar, preserving them in the natural refrigeration of the cellar by covering them with water-glass—

a slimy solution of water and sodium silicate.

She picked wild mint along the brook and made jelly. She could live for days on peanut butter and apples. She bought a sewing machine in town and took the several lessons the shop offered with such a purchase. She then made some of her own clothes, cutting out and pinning patterns on the kitchen table. Beyond the immediate savings, she was tall, without an extra pound, and what selection there was in the local stores was never on sale. She made a coat from a bolt of woolen cloth brought up to Maine by one of my father's relatives. She must have had some help tailoring it, or she was a very quick study indeed. I'm certain it wasn't warm enough for those winter mornings on playground duty. She never had a warm hat, or a coat with a hood. One year she went to the State Teachers' Convention wearing a skirt from her sister-in-law and a blouse from her near-eighty-year-old mother. She never complained about those intrusive farming operations, like hatching, that found their way into the kitchen.

"How'd she get along with your father's relatives—her not Jewish and all."

"She was great. As Daddy has written many times, she was quiet, patient, and very perceptive, and usually withheld judgment. She was the only one who could handle his father."

Muriel. 1933

"Why did she have to handle him?"

"He had been an abusive monster. Daddy hated him, and he could infuriate my father nearly to the point of violence. When Zaide came— "

"Who's Zaide?"

"Yiddish for grandfather. Their truce only lasted a couple of days, and then he would do something or say something or assume something that would set my father off, and an unbreakable silence would descend. At one point during one of these ice-hardened standoffs, my father suggested that they simply leave, but my mother refused to be driven out of her own home. Communication—one way only—was limited to small pieces of paper with some grocery needs scribbled on it, left, early in the morning, under the windshield wiper of the car. My mother was the only one around who could restore civility at any level."

"How'd she do that?"

"Not sure. I think she went over to his little house and spoke to him directly."

"Why'd your father even set him up with a place to live?"

"God! I have no idea. Much later I asked my cousin why on earth Daddy agreed to and then assisted in the actualization of the plan to allow his father to live on our property. She said that after Zaide's mugging, Daddy took him to be a frail, old man, instead of the tyrant he had always been. I don't agree—I think it was money."

"Why money?"

"Because his father was always allowing as how, if such-and-such didn't happen, he would leave all his money to Israel. And Daddy was painfully aware that his family, and particularly his wife, had suffered a great deal. He felt compelled by the promise of money. In either case, he was wrong. His father was still a tyrant, and Daddy never got any money."

"So he left it to Israel?"

"No, I think he left it to a four-year-old grandson. Four was the maximum age that someone could be and not piss him off."

Even this my mother had to suffer, this quelling of her impossible father-in-law's childish behavior and the self-effacement attendant to having to go over and speak to him.

"So how did he get his little house?"

"On, my God! What a story. At some point $800 or thereabouts arrived unsolicited, underscoring the fact that the request that my father 'find him a place to live' was now an outright order, an order whose financial strictures precluded any easy solution. As Zaide had no car, he had to be fairly close by. Daddy finally located a small house somewhere near Augusta. Maybe Monmouth? Hired a guy and the necessary crew to jack up the house where it stood and slide a flatbed trailer under it. Here it comes down Western Avenue in Augusta. But they found themselves blocked by the overpass to the beginning of the Maine Turnpike. So here they are with a house, with an oversized rig without a permit—just him and the driver. Things must have seemed pretty grim—and the trip was far from over. Five miles, including an uncomfortably narrow bridge, lay between them and home. But a cop—he must have gotten help directing traffic—instead of giving them a ticket, stopped traffic and allowed the truck to back up and go under the bridge on the wrong side of a divided highway, as the lay of the land was such that there the clearance was greater. Although temporary, I'm sure seeing the gable of that little building slide out from under the bridge was nearly hallucinatory."

"Were there any other good days you remember?"

"Certainly the happiest event of those years, other than my mother getting up and walking again after her paralysis, was leaving his job at the Augusta State Hospital. He hated that place, and when he tried to organize the hospital orderlies, they didn't have much affection for him, either. Anyhow, he jotted down the following valedictory on the back of his last paycheck. My mother was aghast:"

Christmas is coming,
The geese are getting fat,
Please to put a dollar in the supervisor's hat.
If you haven't got a dollar,
A half dollar will do,

If you haven't got a half dollar,
God damn you!

"They never said anything?"

"Not that I know of. Anyway, back to the move. The rest of the trip passed without too much more excitement, except for several utility wires that had the misfortune of being too low. Now the truck is at the house. First thing the driver has to do is turn the rig around and point it up the hill, then jackknife the trailer with the house on it down a bit of an embankment, and ease the house off the back, blocking it up as it slid off.

Several days later we started digging five-foot holes for supports at each corner—had to be done by hand as there was not enough room for an excavator. Into the holes went Sono-Tubes; they, having been leveled and plumbed, were held in place by back-filling the holes with the same dirt we had shortly before shoveled out. That done, we filled the Sono-Tubes with concrete—yet again by hand. Several days later we gingerly let down the house on them.

You can see what kind of problems are already built into this one-sided transaction, and his father hadn't even seen the house or its site. He would just 'assume' that this was done—he kept the work invisible, lest he might have to offer to pay for it. Then electricity and running cold water. A privy. And of course, when he saw it, it was too little for too much money, and done wrong. Small thanks my father got, and no thanks to my mother, who had to keep him emotionally able to function. It's my mother I don't understand."

"How do you mean?"

"She knew how much Daddy hated him, and how impossible the old man was to live with. Yet she let it happen. She did not normally put her foot down and insist. But she also had been protecting him since the day they met, and preventing this move was most definitely in the category of protecting him—from himself. It was she who would have to mediate their irremediably-toxic father-son relationship—so why didn't she just say no? Daddy might have argued, but he would have caved."

"Did you ever ask her?"

"No, that and a million other things. She took them all with her."

My father learned whatever necessity dictated: plumbing, electrical, sweating copper pipe joints, concrete, moving buildings, raising goats, trapping raccoons, welding, and the thousand one-off jobs that need to be done in an old, country house. But all these things were not accomplishments; they were external to him and so remained valueless, except for their utility. He made precise models in clay to help visualize solid geometry problems. He tutored high-school kids—it was Sputnik time, and at times demand for his help in science and math was more than he could fit into his schedule.

I remember one student—French Canadian, I think—senior in high school. He was naturally quick and mechanically very competent and had already been accepted into an Air Force training program. He was working at the pulp mill, at the top of the log-delivery conveyor. He dropped his pulp hook, and, trying to retrieve it, lost his balance momentarily and stepped onto the steel conveyor. In an instant the front of one of his feet was a bloody mush. He decided to go to college, having paid a draconian price for the opportunity—the mill paid. But he was not ready for engineering school. My father tutored him and brought him along, course by course, and off he went to UMaine. I wonder if he ever realized the depth of the man who was his tutor.

The story involves an amazing coincidence: Only a few years before, my father had been at the bottom of the SAME conveyor, helping a neighbor from Center Montville unload pulpwood. He also lost his pulp hook, but they only had to call to those at the top to watch out for it. They snagged it and tossed it down. My father was mortified at the loss.

He had relearned (I don't think he actually forgot) after twenty-five years or more, Latin, physics, chemistry, calculus.

Submerged in a land in which he was invisible, his knowledge circulated in a vacuum of self-doubt and existed without validation.

We never did get running hot water—not even in the bathroom, but the bathtub stayed cleaner than in most houses.

A sense of duty, a sense of necessity, rather than a goal, pervaded all these things. Except to live through the next year with each other and to maintain their inner sense of values, they had no personal goals. Maybe they had goals for their children, but parents' goals forgone become very heavy for small shoulders. Lives forgone are unbearable.

Chapter XXVIII

Slaughter

The ducks and geese born in the spring were now big and fat, shoveling in corn twice a day as fast as we could pour it into the troughs. Only a few of the best were spared to become part of the breeding stock. In addition to those we raised, we also dressed those of others, whether one or two raised as pets at someone's house out on the lake or a truckload from the Maine State Prison Farm in Thomaston. Killing and plucking a goose: fifty cents; a duck, thirty cents. Accepting someone's pets for slaughter required solemn sighs and knowing looks, meant to signal your recognition of life's brevity and its difficult moral issues. We always offered to swap them bird for bird so they would never have to eat an animal which only last week had a name. A few pheasants; a few guinea fowl. We drew the line on chickens, though I don't know why. A chicken was a snap compared to a well-insulated waterfowl—a little scalding and you could just wipe off the feathers. Didn't have to wax them.

A few hunters came with their mangled Canada geese and limp wild ducks, brought down in a blaze of shotgun fire somewhere in the salt marshes on the coast. The ducks—mallards, teal, clownish-looking wood ducks—were still beautiful in death, luminescent greens with marvelous details of white and blue and grey. Some had broken limbs, others vicious looking bruises. Birdshot had breached their organs, causing them to bleed internally, or worse, their guts had been opened up—real casualties. Having sat around without refrigeration for several days while the hunt went on, they were well ripened. Hence evisceration was a particularly unpleasant job, made even more so by the raw ends of shattered ribs waiting for a water-softened hand. For hunters, word of mouth was all we needed—no need to advertise. We charged little enough for taking an ugly and frustrating job off their hands, with the added benefit that they would then bring home something that looked like food, rather than some creature barely rescued from the talons of an eagle. The ducks were so tiny and naked when dressed—pathetic, really, in terms of food value. One might be an appetizer. They are small flying machines—all feathers and hollow bones.

I feel a redemptive value in animals, more so in wild animals, and most particularly in beautiful wildness. I would like to talk to them, but it would be more emotionally useful if they recognized our appreciation, or if they were more aware of their own beauty. Instead, leading lives of unexamined utility, they flash by. All we are left with is the thrill of recognition. When you see a teal, it is the very essence of teal-ness, for in its life there are only two states: teal and non-teal. We often spend our entire lives groping around looking for ourselves and are condemned not to know it even when we stumble across it. But a teal never gropes, never stumbles. A teal does not need the luxury of fixing the past, because it has the greatest luxury of all: it has the luxury of being what it is, instead of what it might be.

He first started slaughtering in a dark, miserable corner of the unheated barn.

I see him standing amid a shadowy jumble of cast-off containers and jury-rigged equipment, equipment pressed into service in such a foreign environment that to believe it truly usable in its new function was an act of will.

Our first formal slaughterhouse was the chicken coop out by the road, which the chickens had abandoned years before. When we first started helping, I could walk around without paying much attention; soon though, like Jeb and Daddy, I had to stoop—lack of attention caused my head to collide with a rafter, an event made more likely by the building's steep roof and low side-walls. Floors uneven, walls uninsulated, door sagging and drafty, not a window—even in a land where rural poverty was often invisible, it was an object of pity. My father spruced it up a bit and painted it on the inside. Standing on a low platform, I worked much of the day with my hands at better-than-shoulder height, since the only available place to attach hangers were the rafters.

"What'd these hangers look like?"
"The bottoms looked like large paperclips of varying sizes, welded together edge-to-edge on a frame, and arranged in ordered pairs. You selected a pair that was large enough for the bird's legs to go in, but small enough to prevent the feet from slipping through."

My brother worked one side of the bird, I worked the other. Paint or no, it was a vile place to work; in the winter, a Gulag.

The slaughterhouse produced a number of ugly jobs, of which nothing topped having to reclaim the wax used to finish the birds. The wax was recycled by reheating the peelings in a tub and, when fully liquid, straining the accumulated feathers out of it. After skimming all he could from the surface, Daddy poured the rest into a doubled burlap bag (one inside another), and then, by hand, wrung out all the wax he could through this cheese-cloth-like filter. What was left, a smelly, unpleasant mass of wax and cooked feathers, was allowed to harden in the bag and then both were thrown out. The wax was a combination of beeswax and paraffin. It was sold by the pound and came in blocks looking like squares of very dense, butterscotch fudge.

We almost lost this crude abattoir when, reclaiming a tub of wax, my father briefly went into the house: the wax boiled over onto the open gas flame, and smoke started billowing out the door. My brother spotted it and raised the alarm; my father ran, turned off the propane from the outside, and contrary to any reasonable course of action, charged into the building and doused the fire.

Wrung out by inadequacy and self-doubt, he was always getting it wrong, saving those things which poverty required, while those things which were greatly to be valued were invisible, because they were too painful to see.

Fifty-five-gallon drums of congealed blood and others of offal waited stoically alongside the plant until Daddy had time to take them to the Augusta Tallow Company. If I went with him—the family station wagon loaded with waterfowl guts of a certain age—seeing the pitiless face of death would have been welcome in comparison to being seen by someone from school; even seeing some kid I didn't know was agony.

State agricultural inspectors had been coming around every year, getting more and more insistent that we "upgrade" the current place or build a new one, one that would at least acknowledge that there were state standards for slaughtering operations, like running water, for instance. Smoke damage and a scorched building were painfully obvious on their next visit. Their patience finally ran out: "Fix it up or close it up."

So in the summer of 1957 we built a new slaughterhouse. The cement floor and the cement block walls of the new place gave it the ambiance of a bomb shelter. In fairness though, it's floor was level, and in the middle of it was a drain; there were windows, and the walls were full height. For $5 the State gave us a license.

This slaughterhouse was the only "from the ground up" new thing they ever had in Augusta, yet it was something that neither of them really wanted. It stood for fifty-five years, a monument to monumental failure, wasted years, and wasted talent, and the only part of that miserable little farm still standing after the fire that leveled the house and the barn.

Entry was by way of a painted double-wide door; a large kerosene stove provided heat. The day's victims sat in wooden crates outside the door, each crate holding ten to fifteen birds. We staged the crates into the plant as the previous crate was removed, except when it was very cold, in which case one crate was warming up while those already warm went to the knife. The crate had a spring-loaded trapdoor on the top, which opened by pushing it sideways, thus disengaging the door from the fixed pin that held it shut. You endeavored to grab the bird by the legs, clapping your other hand on the wings as soon as possible to prevent bruises caused by thrashing—all the while guarding against potential escapees. The neck, of course, was more readily available, but grabbing it put you at risk of getting raked by the bird's sharp toenails. The geese might register their displeasure at being held by the neck by repeatedly slapping you on the forearm with the bony forward joint of a wing.

If we only had a few birds, we often used burlap bags instead of crates. Getting the birds out of a bag one at a time required skill and speed. Keeping the mouth of the bag closed around your arm, like Polyphemus with Odysseus's men, you felt around blindly until you chanced on some reasonable part of a bird's anatomy. Removing the bird, however, invariably showed those still inside some daylight, and fifteen pounds of determined goose can be pretty convincing. Frightened and totally disoriented, fear gave them wings, although as a rule they were too fat and happy to fly. They might land on your shoulder, at which point you could get a stinging right cross on the side of your head.

When captured, animals stop struggling for a bit, seeming to calm down, to give up, resigned to their fate. This is a ruse. As soon as they feel the capturer relax a little, they pick their moment and, tightly coiled, explode in muscled fury, every ounce of strength put into a last-ditch effort to escape. If you are the capturer and you have relaxed, you have made a mistake.

The unfortunate candidate went head down through a tapering metal cone, whose high, smooth sides were meant to make it impossible for the bird to launch itself backwards (literally, straight up in the air) and escape. Several of these cones, side by side, were positioned over a large trough-like affair, canted slightly so that the blood flowed toward one end, through a hole, and thence into a barrel. But some did not give up their lives so easily. For these, Daddy had sash weights diabolically fitted with hooks.

Using a knife whose image to this day produces a dread and is capable of inflicting the most vicious somatic damage, he cut the bird's throat by first creating a space with his fingers between the windpipe and the aorta as close to the head as possible. Thus holding the head, he inserted the knife and cut backwards. Holding the head, blood spurting out onto his arm, he reached down into the trough and fished out a sash weight from the bloody pool and ran its hook through the soft part of the bird's bottom bill. A type of murder. Blood dripped into the barrel and gelled. The gurgling squawks became weaker and then stopped. I could return to trying to sing the theme from the first movement of *Harold in Italy*.

"He was a real killer . . ."

"Yes, Diane pointed this out several times when I was talking about being afraid of him. He could get scary angry. Daddy admits, with great regret—he is never one to let himself off easily—to having hit Jeb with his fist, who, in the process of pulling back trying to avoid the blow, hit his head on a newel post. Daddy thought he had driven him over the edge—mental breakdown. And then the electric shock incident confirmed it."

"What electric shock incident?"

"Awful. Jeremy put his hand on the pump, and casually (or absentmindedly) extended his hand toward the stove, and *Pow!* he got a real shock. Daddy thought Jeb had lost it—that he was going to lose his favorite son. When Jeb insisted that the shock was real, Daddy tried it. It was no hallucination. Seems the technician from Stone and Cooper, when installing the new dryer in the back hall, had grounded it to the plumbing system instead of to a real ground. It was a world before lawsuits, but the company gave us free gas for the rest of the winter."

"Did he ever hit you?"

"Yes, a few times. I developed a terrific strategy: if I thought I was going to be hit, I dropped to the floor, prone. What could he do, hit me when I'm down already? But the fear extended to much more benign, even perfectly normal, interactions: I remember wanting to drop my subscription to *Boy's Life* and subscribe to an archery magazine, and being afraid to ask his permission."

Four tubs made from ingeniously reworked washing machines stood along the far wall, heated by gas burners. At this distance it seems we got everything at the junkyard—imagination and an acetylene torch can solve a lot of problems, and cheaply too.

When other kids spoke of getting something at the junkyard, it was a mark of status: finding, bargaining, extracting, refitting, fixing something which without that junked part was unfixable. When we went to the junkyard, it was a personal visit to Hell.

The first two tubs contained hot water (one could be changed and heating while the other was in use), the third molten wax, the fourth plain water. We needed two hot-water tubs because on big days the water got dirty, resulting in less effective scalding. Held by the head and feet, my father swished the now-dead bird around in the hot water until the feathers loosened—he never needed a thermometer. He could maintain the water temperature by feel and performance. He added soap to the water to cut through the natural oil present on all waterfowl feathers. My brother and I received the dripping bird, hung it by its legs, judiciously let it cool, and pulled off the feathers. Feathers were of varying value, so we kept the down separate from the large wing- and tail-feathers, the goose down separate from the duck down, and finally the grey goose down separate from the white—all this achieved by swapping out individual bushel baskets. Cleaned of all but fluff, we hung the now-denuded birds in a row along the side-wall. And so the production went, until we had killed and removed the feathers from the last bird of the day.

The third tub contained the molten wax. Starting with the first bird of the day, which was now dry and cool, my father dipped the bird into the wax and then into the water to harden it, repeating these steps until a layer of malleable wax, about the thickness of a shirt cardboard, covered the entire bird except for its head and feet. Wax temperature was critical: too hot and each layer was too thin, requiring the dipping process to be repeated too many times; too cool and too much was used for each bird. Again, with a bird hung on the hanger from the leg joints, Jeremy and I waited until the wax was at the peak of its holding power and then peeled it from the bird, leaving it glistening and feather free. Too soft? The wax pulled away from the feathers. Too brittle? We had to pick the wax off in small pieces like the shell of an uncooperative hard-boiled egg. The used wax went into a bushel basket for the later reclaiming, the operation which had doomed the chicken-coop abattoir.

If the birds were going to a butcher, they were finished: the butcher wanted to do his own eviscerating. This was the exception—most people wanted theirs "oven-ready." Starting again from the first bird, my brother and I removed any remaining pinfeathers (immature feathers) using a strawberry huller and passed them off to my father, who cut off the head and feet. He made a long incision the length of the neck and pulled the skin free, then severed the neck near the body with a cleaver, keeping the skin as a flap to wrap around the back and keep things presentable. Starting at the breastbone, he cut a large slit into the body cavity, being careful not to cut into the guts, and forced his hand in and around the mass of internal organs, working carefully to loosen the tough connective tissue holding them in place. The ideal was to remove the entire body contents intact, and in one sure motion. He cut the heart and gizzard free, then, gently holding the liver clear, cut around the bile sac. The rest of the guts went into the barrel for the offal company. He then cut open the gizzard from the side, as you would a bagel, except not all the way through: this was less easy than it might seem, the gizzard being tough and slippery, while your hands were wet and slippery, and the table coated with fat and body juices.

Occasionally we found corroded nails embedded in the gizzard— forget it, just cut away that part, or dump the whole thing. Wash out any gravel and remaining bits of food, then peel off the tough inner lining. Sometimes the lining came off in one piece, other times you picked at it for five minutes.

Everything was so turned in, so self-referential, so socially unusable. Is it like that in families everywhere? Quickly peeling off the inner lining of a gizzard, and in one continuous piece, is an accomplishment, properly a piece of ego-money, saved up to be spent as needed. Outside, however, it was an unrecognized currency—as was everything else—unrecognized, or secret, or both: their lives, their politics, their accomplishments, their pasts. So impermeable was this self-imposed cocoon, and such, as a consequence, was the pneumatic pressure exerted on those inside, that the informal, the spontaneous, or the unstructured never flourished.

When my brother and I first started, we could bail out on the eviscerating; Daddy had to do it all. As we got older, we were required to help, and the various eviscerating jobs were parceled out according to age and ability. First the gizzards, then cutting away all the giblets, then the evisceration itself. At some point Daddy started to pay us for every bird slaughtered, and more for every bird eviscerated. Hours went by. When finished with the evisceration, we rinsed the bird in cold water, wrapped up the giblets and the neck in butcher wrap paper, and inserted this neat package into the body cavity. We were finished. A real showpiece: there was nothing like them in the whole state, maybe in the whole country. A free-range (before it was all the rage), plump, grain-fed bird, no antibiotics, no steroids, raised and finished by hand. Daddy sold the geese for seventy-five cents a pound.

Early in the season we could get out of there by noon. As Thanksgiving approached and the weather got colder, the work days got longer. At the end of the day, most of which was spent standing in rubber boots, I was nearly soaked to the waist, my hands wrinkled and softened by constant contact with water, and my nails pulled away from the quicks from picking wax, picking pinfeathers, picking gizzard linings. It was painful to scrape the back of my hand on the sharp ridges of a bird's ribcage as I tried to loosen the insides.

Madness reigned before Thanksgiving. We stayed out of school for several days, several long days, to help, because everyone wanted theirs "fresh." We ran out of storage room in the slaughterhouse; the overflow got piled in various places around the house, back again, in death, like the plague. Barrels of guts waited patiently.

How was it that I didn't have to bathe after a day like that? Wash my hands and face in the kitchen sink before I went to bed—that's it. Miraculously, I never smelled. We never did have a shower.

Christmas saw the end of it. The geese had finished getting fat. The iron sharpness of the cold grabbed me when I went out with my brother, clothes and hands wet, to get the next crate. Baskets of soaking wet feathers weighing forty pounds froze solid. Because the kerosene stove had no blower, the air did not circulate: high up it was eighty degrees; at your feet it was forty. Opening the double doors to bring in a crate let in a blast of arctic air. This, as with many things, was converted from a hardship to a virtue: what with the kerosene stove and the human beings and the gas burners and the heavy-breathing waterfowl, the oxygen in the place got low, and opening the doors to the frozen morning replenished it. Another bump in the road made smooth by necessity.

Through those dreary days I looked forward to the wonderful treat in store for us when we got through the holidays and the slaughtering finally ended for the season: a bottle of ginger ale and a half-gallon of vanilla ice cream. It was homemade ice-cream-soda time, and you got to use the biggest glass you could find! Each slurp of the melting ice cream and the fizzy ginger ale was nearly hallucinatory.

When my father was on shift work at the State Hospital, he had to change his sleeping routine fairly frequently—something he found difficult. We had a party line, and the telephone would disturb him; in the summer the whippoorwills drove him nearly mad. In this particular incident, he awoke and decided that our old radio was the offending party, came downstairs, yanked it out of the wall, and smashed it. This despite the fact that it was on so low we had to sit close just to hear it, and despite it being downstairs, and despite it being at the other end of the house. I would sit motionless listening to *The Green Hornet* or *The Lone Ranger*, heart pounding, body rigid with excitement, bladder at emergency levels, holding my urethra closed because I was unwilling to take a bathroom break. In the middle of one of our many days in the slaughterhouse, he expressed regret over that outburst, and allowed as how that old tube radio would have been a nice thing to have to relieve the tedium.

But if he had really wanted a radio, any old secondhand radio would have done. But he had no interest in radio or their typical programming. He wanted "that" radio, as if it was an unusual artifact of the past, as if its destruction left a "hole" in the fabric that kept his life together.

Chapter XXIX

Fencing

We ran fencing around the place to keep the ducks and geese from wandering onto the neighbors' property. Web-footed couch potatoes, too fat to fly except *in extremis*, they always came home—they knew where the grain was.

We used six-foot untreated cedar fence posts, spaced every ten or twelve feet. By repeatedly slamming down a twelve-pound crowbar, we made a narrow vertical hole, rotating the top of the crowbar to widen the diameter some. Small rocks could be pushed aside; bigger ones had to be dug out of the ground. Really big ones were left. We could have used dynamite, but instead we took the easier route and simply fenced around them. The post, sharpened with an axe and driven home with the side of a sledge, stuck out of the ground about four feet. Every once in a while we reinforced a post by putting angled braces on both sides in line with the pull of the fencing; this bracing had to be done on corners also. The posts in and the end of the galvanized fencing attached to the starter post, one person stretched the wire as taut as possible, the second braced the post against the hammer blows by putting his shoulder against it, and the third hammered in the fence staples. None of us had it easy. The stretcher could not evenly apply tension across the width of the fencing, causing sags; the one who absorbed the hammer blows did just that, each blow feeling like the kick of a thirty-thirty—

a rifle with a bore of .3030 of an inch—

but without the thrill; and quickly hammering staples into a round post of dried cedar, a post that bounces some with every hammer blow, is not as easy as one might think. The work was slow and frustrating, particularly along quick changes in elevation.

For temporary fences we used the painfully-acquired crates—

"Remind me. Why were they painful?"

"Because we stopped at the grocery stores in town and took home their boxes of spoiled vegetables."

These crates were about three feet wide, and consisted of open, wired-together, wooden slats. Undoing a couple of connecting wires and knocking out the ends gave you a flexible, five-foot length of construction potential. Stand them on edge, wire them together, attach the ends securely, put a post behind it once in a while so it won't get pushed over, and you have a temporary fence, effective as long as the birds stayed on the ground. Again, way ahead on the recycling curve!

We made two bridges across the brook—upstream from the dam, but still on our property. The piers were made by piling up rocks; the walkways were of planks salvaged years before from the destruction of that rickety shed between the house and the barn. They were fun to walk on, springy but strong. Why two bridges? I don't know—one would have sufficed to get over to the small, mean, piece of land on the other side. We at some point attempted to mow over there, since we now had a way to get the machine across easily. It was a useless exercise.

Peter Mills, Henry. Augusta, 1957.

Part VI

Winter

The snow softens the landscape, easing transitions, filling depressions; its monochromatic pervasiveness is a key to winter's oppression. Ice hides all but the fastest water in the brook; during severe cold snaps, even the spillway water freezes, a striated, glistening arc. In the gardens, only an occasional stalk pokes through the whiteness. Some farmers, deliberately or otherwise, leave round bales in the field; their tan, hunched backs knuckle up through the snow. The cold isolates each house, reducing mobility to essential trips, reducing neighborliness to a wave of the hand. Each house gets through the winter on its own. As the embankments of snow at the sides of the road grow, it is no longer possible to see other cars at intersections. At noon, the sun lies low in the south—the low-angle light foreshortens the white landscape and hardens the outlines of buildings. By two p.m. the shadows grow very long; darkness comes at four. The cold hardens. In the morning a cardinal or a jay might alight on a bare limb outside our window—a thrilling flash of intense color. If you walk through an orchard, you might find a puffball,

a rotten apple with brittle skin and dust inside,

hanging on an otherwise bare tree. One squeeze, one cloud of grey-brown "smoke" is all you get; then the fun is over. We often saw animal tracks in the snow, and hastened to identify them with loud overconfidence. The roadside snacks were gone—the only thing available possibly, if you were down at Tommy's, was a piece of fermented ensilage on a cold, boring afternoon.

Chapter XXX

Winter Fun

Turcotte's house sat at the top of the highest hill on the road. Behind it was a hill of such length and steepness that a toboggan on hard crusted snow nearly reached escape velocity. On our two-man toboggan we attempted to steer by edging it, leaning in unison, or occasionally dragging a foot. Either usually had the effect of simply making the toboggan come about, which hardly improved control, since now we were going backwards. Control was critical for a long run, as some distance up from the foot of this hill ran a thin row of bushes and small trees sheltering a stone wall, with only a narrow opening in it for farm machinery to pass. Toward this opening, of course, we attempted to steer. When totally out of control, or having given up all hope of getting through, we bailed off at the last possible minute to avoid being catapulted into the trees. Digging into the snow, we slowed ourselves enough to avoid getting hurt; meanwhile the empty toboggan banged harmlessly against the rocks and bushes. We recovered our much-abused friend and slogged back up for another run.

On the other side of the road from this high point was an even steeper, although much shorter, hill. It was bare ledge, and in the winter the water that ran down it froze, a bobsled run without the high walls. Riding a sled down the naked ice was a near-death experience, the trees at the bottom growing exponentially larger every second, the sled's narrow, metal runners chattering, eyes tearing, the sled bucking over the icy bumps, nearly out of control. A frozen face and cold hands were minor inconveniences. We lived for another run: next time we should try two on one sled! And then there was going into town with Allen Farnum's father to go bowling—

"You went bowling? Where'd you go?"
"I think we went to the YMCA. He picked us up in his panel truck,

and we rode in the cold dark, sitting on whatever was in the back of his van."

"How'd you do?"

"We didn't actually get to bowl much. Most of the time was spent watching the bowling league players, or maybe we reset the pins? I'm no longer sure. This was candlestick bowling—small balls. Then, league play finished, we got to throw a few of our own. The most fun was being away from the house."

"Yes, it doesn't sound like these were your most memorable evenings. You guys have any spruce trees?"

"Yeah. They were all over."

"Could you chew the gum?"

"Oh, God. Spruce gum and fiddlehead ferns. Every season produced at least one breathless discussion of the wonderful qualities of spruce gum. I don't know, maybe we had the wrong variety of spruce, or the wrong sex trees. The hardened spruce gum we pulled off the local trees tasted like a soft piece of bathroom disinfectant dipped in kerosene."

"Well, the kids who might have actually chewed it—where did they get it?"

"They bought it, but even the spruce gum you bought in a box took a bit of getting used to. When you first put it in your mouth, it was hard like a piece of candy. Bite down on it, and your mouth was filled with sprucey dust, only coalescing into a wad after getting thoroughly wet with saliva."

"You tried it?"

"Yeah. I just about spit it out, but hung on, and it finally turned into gum. They're right, the flavor never does go away, but your jaws get tired after a while because its resilience also never goes away—kind of like chewing on a piece of spruce-flavored Spaldini."

"And a Spaldini is?"

"A high-bouncing rubber ball the size of a tennis ball but without the flocking."

A few nights of below zero temperatures produced a layer of ice on the brook of sufficient thickness to allow safe skating. This skating lasted until the first heavy snowstorm.

"What happened when it snowed?"

"We didn't want to shovel sufficient space to skate on the brook— that was a lot of work, and unless done immediately, snow makes the surface of the ice crunchy instead of hard and smooth—so we were forced to other places."

"You mean places that could flood the rink?"

"Yeah, that, or places with large ice scrapers or a small tractor."

"What were the ice scrapers?"

"Ice scrapers were rectangles of moderately stiff metal, roughly 2' × 5', with 5' long wooden handles extending from the short sides. These, powered by a skater on each handle, were driven plow-wise across the ice, clearing a large swath with each pass. Hitting an immovable bump in the frozen surface caused the snow scraper to come to an abrupt halt, while the drivers ended up on the ice, unable to handle the instantaneous deceleration."

"That still sounds like a lot of work. Where'd you go to get warm?"

"The best places had a warming hut, a rough, smoky building with wooden benches, a wooden floor to save your skate blades, and a place to buy snacks. Like a recess playground, they were filled with noisy kids, all of whom seemed to be hanging out with friends and having the most outrageously good time. More importantly, the hut provided a place to put on your skates, an unpleasant task with bare hands at twenty degrees."

I entered such places with a certain dread, for in any group of kids I was always at the periphery—as Marlow so tellingly said of Jim, "a straggler yearning inconsolably for his humble place in the ranks." Except once, Yes! Except once, when Pam extended her hand to me and asked, "Do you want to skate with me?" Round and round we went. What we might have talked about is lost, but I'm sure my side was a lumpy slurry of the obvious and the socially inept, delivered in the sophisticated English that I heard at home. Years later she told me that I was one of the smartest kids—"in a different league," I think is how she put it.

"So you liked skating?"

"I hated skating. I hated sports. I hated music. I hated everything in that bisexual world that I was forced to inhabit."

"Were you worried that you were bisexual?"

"Bisexual? I didn't know bisexual from Newton's Second Law of Thermodynamics. I couldn't have been bisexual, I didn't know sexual. But I was emotionally bisexual. Hell, I was so confused that I failed to pass the Army Security Agency's standard lie-detector test. I was leaving the Army anyway, so it was not a big issue, but they wouldn't give me a 'Secret' clearance, and 'Secret' is so nothing: how many jars of peanut butter the mess hall has is probably Secret."

"You have to talk about this so bluntly? Isn't there a more appropriate time? What will your children think?"

"They can think whatever they want. And the time is long since gone. And what do you find here inappropriate?"

"Whyn't you let everyone stay comfortable with your own carefully crafted myth. This is going to make everybody squirm."

"Let 'em squirm: living it is a kind of death; and the myth is mostly just pleasant myopia on their part ..."

"Okay, okay. So what does 'emotionally bisexual' mean exactly?"

"It means—Christ! what does it mean? It means I couldn't be like my mother, because I was a boy, and I couldn't be the girl they both wanted. My father took Jeb to be his favorite, a position my brother held as an inalienable sinecure. I couldn't be a writer because he never invited me in. And I couldn't be a musician because I had little interest and less talent—"

"But you played for years, and you played first-chair cello at All-State and—

"You interrupted me—I wasn't finished. I said it in my poem, *The First Bridge:* 'For to the one I do not want, and to the other I am not wanted. The dam beckons.' And music? My interest was a sham, and the hundreds of hours—"

"Hundreds?"

"Actually more like thousands—of practicing a waste of time, or time I couldn't spend figuring out what I might actually want. Performances and concerts were dreaded. It was a slow form of torture, the last event unsatisfactory because I was not yet a star, the next event looming with uneasiness and despair. And then I traded in my senior year at Cony for Rochester—I can't believe I did that. Music was like a sacrifice left at the feet of some implacable god—actually a sacrifice for masculinity."

"When did you figure out you hated everything?"

"I have always known hate, even when I didn't know it. And every day, every hour, that hate lies in wait, and the punishment for that hate— *fantasy of castrating myself with a sharp skate-blade*—sits on me like a somatic poltergeist. I have this vague but persistent memory of being outside, near my mother, somewhere in back of the house in Center Montville—maybe she was gardening? Might have been an apple tree nearby. I did something that a three-year-old who is full of himself would do. She laughed. And that was the last time I did something where I was able to invest my entire being. That was the last time it went right. But it was also the place where it went very wrong."

"How do you mean?"

"It was there on some day that fall when my father burned the manuscript of his aborted novel—the one he started in California. Jeremy and I watched it burn. By report, we were amused."

"Awful. Such a personally destructive act, itself a castrating act. And now?"

"Things are better, thanks to Diane and a lot of work—years of work. And it's much better when I'm writing. But I'm still sad about the past— so smart, so talented, so good-looking, so charming, so well-spoken . . . And so little accomplished. Except I did learn how to love my children without condition. For all those years I was two people: the one who acted in the world in some 'normal' fashion, the way he thought others expected, or the way he thought might please, and the subducted one, the hidden one, the one almost nobody saw, the one who siphoned off my emotional energy and attention, the one who watched me live. I became my father, who, as I pointed out earlier, also watched himself live."

"Phooey! You're just posturing. You did so much better than your father, in stability, in your family, in your self-confidence, in your health . . ."

"Oh sure. I avoided some of his most scandalous failings, particularly maybe the sexual. I skinned by homosexuality, but not by much. But I was like him—not too surprising, huh? That's all I ever wanted. How could I do anything? I was continually splitting my resources."

"So you managed to escape?"

"Escape? Yes, in a sense. Rescued may be more like it. Remember that although Ishmael was rescued, he never escaped—there was none."

"When did you quit the hated music? You still play anything now?"

"No. I remember we were walking somewhere in Rochester, in town—graduation weekend, Brighton High School. I remember the day was warm, warm but gritty and very small and we walked along the lumpy sidewalk, just Daddy and me and Mommy trailing somewhere behind, walking next to where they were putting in the foundation for the new concert hall, raw and cavernous, with its saliva-thickening smell of uncured concrete, and I told him I was done with music, and death became a companion. Anchor gone, I cut myself adrift. I was going to try male things. And I failed."

"What did you try?"

"I enrolled in summer school at the University of Rochester—cynically I say now that it was just to keep me from hanging around the house in Augusta and using the car. Anyway, what did I pick? A Daddy subject: chemistry. I was pathetically unprepared and failed out—nowhere near enough math."

"Speaking of remembering, do you remember that green jacket you used to have, the one with the waffle weave that made it sort of padded, the one that you were wearing that day in Rochester?"

"Yeah, I remember that one—I thought it was great, kind of a soft green, like over-washed Army fatigues. Is that the one you mean?"

"Uh-huh. What did you like about that coat? It was different than other guys might have worn. Leather buttons as I recall. Kind of faggy, wasn't it?"

"I don't know—maybe—but it was sophisticated I thought, and I had picked it out on my own. It was longish—straight—no hips showing with that coat. You know I was still concerned about my figure—always checking my profile to make sure—ya' know—nothing sticking out."

There was another pond on our road where we met friends once or twice each winter. Here we burned old tires; in the utter darkness their bright flames assaulted our eyes. Heedless of the vile black smoke pouring into the air, we toasted marshmallows until they were black, then exposed their white, tender insides by sucking off the burnt sugar, repeating this until there was nothing left but stick. When the fun was over, we sat on a frozen log, took off our skates, slid our cold feet into even colder boots, and walked home.

Fun at home in the winter was difficult—three sort-of-warm rooms, all with poor circulation, low ceilings, and cold floors is not a lot for a family of four. There was nowhere else to go—the unheated rooms had a flat, unappetizing chill, making you want to grab whatever you came for and get out quickly. No one could be home without being, in some sense, underfoot—there was no place that offered both privacy and comfort.

"But where did you practice?"

"I had to practice in the living room, one of the three warm rooms—and I practiced for hours. I'm not sure how they tolerated it. And I never could play very well—wasn't as if I was adding to the ambiance. How could anybody read or concentrate? And my mother had absolute perfect pitch."

"Meaning what?"

"That I could be practicing and she could be working in the garden and call out 'F#!'"

"You couldn't do that?"

"No, I only had relative perfect pitch. I could hear that it was wrong, but I couldn't say how to correct it without looking at the music."

"How boring! There must have been some other stuff to do, besides music and reading. Didn't you have any games?"

"Sure, Parcheesi, Scrabble, cards. We made a carom table to fit on the card table, and flicked those wooden O's with our fingers. Somebody gave us a chemistry set—I never explored it much. Also an inexpensive microscope. I really got into it for a while. I would make six circles on a piece of paper, and then look at salt or a butterfly wing and draw the picture. I remember my mother taking me to the Maine State Entomology Lab near the Augusta State Hospital. We walked around and looked at all the carefully pinned insects. She encouraged me. Didn't work. Not sure why."

"Did your father ever sit with you? You know, like, play?"

"No, but we did get to join him in another exciting, winter event: putting on dark goggles and sitting in a room, mostly naked, bathed in ultraviolet light. He did this as part of some therapy, but for exactly which of his skin maladies I don't remember."

"That's it?"

"I did a lot of daydreaming. Did you ever get those cards out of boxes of Nabisco Shredded Wheat?"

"I don't remember any cards. What'd they look like?"

"Gray cardboard. They used them for packing—to separate the layers of the shredded wheat so it didn't self-shred in shipment."

"Oh, yeah! The ones with the 'Indian Lore' printed on them—how to do stuff."

"Yes, cool stuff, like a portable shower, an archery target made from fat coils of straw, a teepee—they made them seem improbably easy. I built them all. A regular Walter Mitty."

"What else did you build—I mean actually build?"

"I once built an archery target. But generally, I was not allowed to build anything too well. I can tell by the level of self-damage that flows from simply the idea of a creative and successful completion, from even telling you that I can do something well."

"You talk to yourself?"

"All the time. I have whole conversations with people—young people, old people, children, students, other people's children—who are not there—beautifully worded, polished, erudite, interesting, perceptive, cadenced, balanced, historically accurate, logically assembled—need anything else?"

"You are so full of sh--! What are these conversations about?"

"Oh, whatever comes along: that a sushi knife only has one bevel, like a plane iron; how a teenager should say no; how a kid should introduce himself; the different levels of pavement on the Interstate; why waterfowl need to be waxed; why a parent should not say 'everybody'; how using the word 'should' with a child simply increases the power of the Super-Ego; the brilliance of Freud's drawing of the human psyche in *Civilization and Its Discontents*—worth a Nobel prize, but could be reproduced freehand in about ten seconds; what is Smyth sewing; how hydrophobia makes modern printing possible; how rotogravure printing works; what's the best stuff to use in an agricultural backpack sprayer; where to stash water for the climb out when going down to Kenab Creek in the Grand Canyon; what's the surest sign that a spruce is a black spruce; the difficulty of getting big air holes in the bread you bake; visitor information on going to such hot spots in Maine as Ripogenus Dam and Patten; how modern life conspires against maleness; the greatness of Borges; Wagner's use of catachresis in *Tristan und Isolde*; how the mother of Dmitri Mendeleev, the developer of the Periodic Table, took him and his sister and *walked* from Siberia to Moscow, only to be told he could not enter the university because he wasn't Russian; what is Wagner's *Ring* actually about; *Housekeeping*; *Sometimes a Great Notion*; *Lord Jim*; *Moby Dick*; *Within the Context of No Context*; *All That Is Solid Melts Into Air*; *A Mathematician Reads the Newspaper*; *Let Us Now Praise Famous Men*; *A Distant Mirror*; *The Guns of August*; *Daily Life in Ancient Rome*; *The Greek Experience*; *The Origins of the Inquisition in Spain in the Fifteenth Century*; what is first normal form; how to quickly figure out the necessary diameter of a tree to get a 10 x 10 beam out of it; explaining why a sphere is such an efficient way to package something; where the paper for *The New York Times Magazine* comes from; what is elision; what's the difference between a homonym and a heteronym; what is ekphrasis; what did the command 'Stand by to wear ship!' actually mean on a square rigger; where the Tabard Inn isn't; why Vergil must have smiled when he wrote the line: *'quidve dolens regina deum tot volvere casus'*; the best brands of long underwear; using vocabulary cards; filing the rakers from both sides on a chainsaw chain; why, immediate you hear it, you know what the Anglo-Saxon word 'Ðæċ' means; the quick formula to find a close approximation of the distance to the horizon, knowing your altitude; how logarithms work—"

"Okay, okay! I get it. Enough a'ready. Christ! You're all over the place. What bullsh--!"

"No bull. Just me—some of me. I guess not very useful, but . . ."

Chapter XXXI

Heat

The place in Augusta was our first house in Maine with central heating. The furnace was a huge affair; it burned coal, and appeared to be about the size of a Volkswagen: ducts like the branches of a galvanized banyan tree leading to the first-floor radiators; clanging, cast-iron doors at different levels; cleaning grates at the bottom which were rotated by engaging a removable crank, like starting our old Model A. Turning this handle caused cinders and clinkers to rain down into a collection bin and a gritty smoke of fly ash and dust to boil out of the open door. The ashes were shoveled out—more dust—and carried in buckets outside for dumping, yet more dust.

Always be sure to check the wind direction before upending an ash pail—you could end up looking like a chimney sweep in Victorian London!

After several years of coal, whether for financial reasons or esthetic, we moved to slabs, the wood of the impoverished.

"The impoverished? Why the impoverished?"
"Slabs are the edges of the big softwood logs that a sawmill cuts into lumber. The log must be squared before it can produce long lengths of salable boards or timbers. These off-cuts are a nuisance—junk, actually—almost at the level of sawdust, and the mill is happy to get rid of what they don't use for their own heating operations."
"So how cheap are they?"
"I don't remember. They don't cost much—in fact the mill will fill your truck using their front-end loader for a few dollars. The final price is mostly the cost of transportation, and the labor involved in sawing it into stove-length pieces and delivering it to a customer. These slabs are largely pitch and bark and burn quickly while producing creosote,

the flammable pitch that precipitates out of cooling smoke and coats the inside of the chimney, raising the possibility of a chimney fire. After several more years, we moved up to hardwood, a great relief."

"Why? Just because of the creosote business?"

"No, more. It stacked easier, burnt longer, and produced less detritus— the bark on softwood tends to come off in the drying process, and slabs were mostly bark. Before getting the first delivery in the fall we had to clean the floor of the cellar using a snow shovel and a rake."

Ernest delivered several truckloads every fall. A cord of hardwood cut into stove-length pieces and split was $25.

"What actually *is* a cord of wood?"

"It's the standard measure of wood harvesting. Formally a pile of neatly stacked logs four feet high, four feet wide, and eight feet long."

Having skidded out the wood the winter before, he cut it and split it by hand. We pitched it down the bulkhead stairs into the cellar, and proceeded to stack it, floor to ceiling, in every available space, leaving only narrow defiles to get to the canned goods or the electric water pump. These stacks, some of which were free standing, required the sensitivity of a builder of fieldstone walls, where rocks, despite all their variations in size and shape, must be made to fit together in a tightly-locked whole. I was never any good at this, always leaving too many spaces, or making stacks which were out of plumb and so in danger of immanent collapse.

"So what did you do?"

"I brought armfuls of wood, while my brother built the stacks. In several days we had put away all the wood for the winter, and thus we surrounded the burning furnace with its own fuel. All this for generally heating only two rooms—"

"But the first floor of that house had more than two rooms."

"Yes, but the kitchen had no cellar under it, so no possibility of ducts from the furnace, and the other room was left unheated in the winter."

As an aid to character development and to practice being helpful, my brother and I cut wood on winter weekends when the lack of other chores, like shoveling snow, raised the possibility that an adult might have to spend time with us or find us other amusements. Actually, he had all the character he needed, it was mine that was behind the curve, definitely behind, and loosing ground. However, his character did not extend to considerations of empathy, help, or protection. Off we would go on a grey, fifteen-degree afternoon, tromping uncomfortably a mile or more through the snow, carrying several axes, a hatchet and a buck saw. We didn't take the crosscut—

"What's a crosscut?"

"A saw about eight feet long, with 1.5" teeth in a 6" wide blade, and with a short handle on each end—a tool for two strong men and big trees."

We never thought to take snacks or drinks; they were not invented yet. Finding our growing stack of wood, we set to work locating medium-sized hardwood trees. Saw part way into the tree, scarf it with an axe to make it fall in the most advantageous direction (and avoid having it hang up in one of the surrounding trees). Saw into the scarf from the back, and down it came with a heavy swish, burying the bottom limbs in the snow.

Limb the sucker, cut off the top, drag it to the pile, saw it into four-foot lengths, pile it up, find another tree.

In retaliation for being hectored and manipulated into this unnecessary foolishness, he wrote a contract that, disingenuously purring like a kitten, he got me to sign. At the first sign of recalcitrance or lack of enthusiasm on my part, he would take out his contract and wave it around, and get my parents to enforce it! In retaliation I cut my thumb one day. I cut my right thumb, and I am right handed. I cut a two-inch gash in my thumb the long way, a remarkable achievement even for someone so uncoordinated.

Have I told you I wanted to be like my father? He also cut himself while using a hatchet with his left hand.

What was I doing? We walked home. I felt weak several times and wanted to stop. Stopping was not allowed. We made it home. Since the cut had already stopped bleeding and I could move my thumb, the prevailing medical opinion was that I did not need stitches or other medical attention. Another expense successfully avoided. That was the end of our logging operation, since the cost of a trip to the doctor was greater than the value of the wood we cut. But, having grown used to managing me—having, actually, largely stepped into the vacuum created by the always-uneven and often-nonexistent parenting exhibited by the grownups in the house—he was not to be put off so easily. When, on the next appropriate day, my parents refused to enforce the terms of the "contract," in a fit of frustrated rage he put his fist through the glass window of the pantry. Although annoying, because he created work, at least he had the good sense not to cut himself, and so require skilled medical attention.

He was lucky, always lucky. What are the odds that you could put your fist through a pane of glass and come away unscathed? Anyway, I had him now! Whenever he got too bossy, or decided whatever I wanted to do was without merit, I could taunt him saying, "Oh, why don't you put your fist through another window! Maybe this time you will get cut, and everyone will feel sorry for you!" I never did. It never felt good to win. Whenever I had the advantage, I always gave it away as quickly as possible; whenever I had something, I didn't let myself keep it, as if there was a law of nature that said I may not possess. By what right should I possess, seeing that my parents had so little? I have sold myself cheap so as not to appear too valuable, and in consequence devalue those who should love me. I have given away things that were rightfully mine—

"Like what? What was rightfully yours?"

"Like everything, everything ... I was head of the computer department of a small company. The company had contracted with a firm to develop an accounting/inventory control system. What they delivered was full of bugs. I knew something about programming, and about the language in which the system was written, but maybe not enough in the beginning. So instead of working and learning day and night, and getting one-on-one help when necessary, and having the confidence to gain mastery, I recommended that we hire someone. The guy came in wearing a white shirt, except, oops, there was a big coffee stain on the front. He got the job: $500/day. Worked there for seven years. A dirty shirt and he got the job. Or there was a woman that I met, upstairs in this rather grim apartment building on 32nd St., beautiful, tall, great figure, short blond hair, a nurse. She thought I was great. But she was already spoken for, but the speaker was in Thailand and wouldn't be home for a while, but made sure she knew that he was getting all the female services a man might desire. According to her roommate, the guy was a shit. I let her go. I walked away. That's not normal. I should have fought. I might have lost, but, on the other hand, I might have won. There's more, but you get the idea ..."

That winter, Ernest took the pung—

"What, for Christ's sake, is a pung? Where do you get these words?"
"I collect them; 'pung' is only one of thousands."
"You have a private dictionary?"
"Yeah. Anyhow, pung is a localism, and more commonly called a work sledge—a strongly-built platform with four runners instead of wheels and posts in the corners—used to haul heavy loads through the snow."

Having harnessed the horses to the pung, Ernest hauled out our hard-won stash of firewood. We walked up the hill to help him saw it into stove-length pieces. The saw was immovably made, with a cast iron frame, about fifteen feet long, on which sat, at one end, a gasoline engine, and at the other, the saw table. A dangerous machine, even in a dangerous and accident-prone business like logging. My father watched, only a couple of years earlier, a similar saw neatly amputate two of Frank Livingston's fingers. Very neat, he said—cut the fingers off the glove and the fingers off the hand. But here we were. Having started the engine by pouring dry gas or some other explosively combustible fluid into the carburetor, Ernest connected the saw to the power by using his body to force a six-inch-wide canvas belt onto the rotating, exposed, driveshaft of the engine and the twenty-four-inch diameter saw blade came to speed—a naked, snarling, adversary, waiting for you to let your absolute attention wander for one instant. We threw a length of wood on the saw table. Pushing it along until an appropriate length overhung the table, the operator, holding the uncut end firmly, cut off the piece by pushing the table forward. Someone caught the piece thus cut off, hands ten inches from disaster, and threw it on the growing pile or directly into his truck. Sawdust flew in your face; the one-lung, make-and-break engine backfired with explosive ferocity, rippling the cold air.

"What's a make-and-break engine?"
"I found out recently from a guy running old machinery at a wool festival: a mechanism completes (makes) an electrical circuit by mechanically pushing two wires together, then pulls them apart (breaks), and a spark is produced, causing the gas in the cylinder to explode. This mechanism in later machines was, of course, replaced by a spark plug. The timing was poor on this kind of crude device, so the engines tended to backfire."
"When was the last time you helped using this saw?"
"Maybe 1958."
"And when did you find out about how it actually worked?"
"I don't know. 2010 maybe?"

"So you stored up this question for fifty-two years until you found someone who could answer it? You fill your head up with this kind of stuff? No wonder you never did anything noteworthy!"

"You're just jealous because you can't do nothing as cleverly as I can—I've made it an art."

Ernest's truck, a 1932 Ford, had a pleasant side-to-side limberness from age and use, factors which seem to have produced the opposite effect on the springs, giving the truck a tank-like ride that rattled your brains. The exposed rod brakes transferred the brake pedal pressure mechanically rather than hydraulically. This, together with the crank in the front of the truck for emergency starts, brought awe-inspired comments as to its age. He drove down and backed up to the now-open bulkhead. We threw our hard-won stash down the stairs and added it to the inventory for the coming winter.

Chapter XXXII

School

School was awful. There is not one redeeming moment, not one event to which a positive, confident feeling is attached. There is not one class in which I shone. There is not one extracurricular event whose memory is pleasant. There is not one school trip from which it would not have been a relief to have stayed home, and remember, home was not a place where I was happy. I don't remember ever answering a question. I knew nothing. I remember learning only two things. I—

"What two things?"

"Long story—forget it. I only remembered decades later."

"No, no. You brought it up . . ."

"Both were comments from English teachers. Sophomore year: we are reading *A Tale of Two Cities*. Miss Pross, fighting Madame Defarge for her life, but more importantly, the life of her beloved Lucy who is fleeing revolutionary France, starts to cry. The teacher pointed out that she was crying not from sadness or from weakness (but this, of course, is how Defarge read it), but that she was simply overwhelmed by her own emotions. Senior year English, maybe even AP English: We are reading *Lord Jim*. The teacher said that one of Conrad's themes is that man is just not up to the job expected of him. That's it. That's what I remember from four years of torture."

In punishment for thinking about having to repeat any one of them I cut off the fingers of my left hand.

I existed in a fog of doubt, distraction, and dread. I accommodated others' wishes without examining my own, and without examining their agenda. That I had no wishes that were mine is a detail apparently nobody noticed.

I shouldn't be too hard on others: it took me almost fifty years before I noticed it myself. I would gladly take a box cutter and hack myself up rather than revisit those years. Better to have died than even to have to write this.

"So why didn't you commit suicide? You are so full of death."

"I suppose the bravery of my parents, who, despite horrific loses, kept on trudging, kept on loving, or to paraphrase what a friend said about Ivan Karamazov, they kept on keeping on. They were surrounded by pieces of abandoned lives from which they constructed a present of sorts, and they had a long if improbable love affair of fifty years. For a child to have experienced that is today very rare. As people, they may have been wrong, but they were not a fiction. My mother had a lot of courage, and, in retrospect, must have believed that 'tomorrow will be better.' And I'm not big on suffering. I whine . . ."

"But your parents would have been sad!"

"Yes, but they would have gotten over it—just another terrible blow in a life full of them. Then I could have existed in their memories as I never was. Or as I was when I was a baby—my mother used to say I looked like Jesus Christ!"

"Didn't you have any friends?"

"I had a few friends before high school, but at Buker, something strange happened."

Henry and Muriel, 1975.

"What's Buker?"

"The name of the school they built to consolidate all the eighth grades across the city. It wasn't finished by September, so the entire city-wide class, in groups, got farmed out to the various schools around town. At some point we moved to the new school. Pretty chaotic—it was a matter of pride to us that our homeroom went through five teachers in the course of the year. Anyway, at Buker, all the friendships faded quickly. High School? I remember none of them. Puberty was happening to everybody else."

"When was all this?"

"1956-7. Elvis Presley time. I remember a few of the students: Larry Conklin, whom I've already mentioned. And there was a girl—Caroline Solti, very bright evidently, certainly pretty and put together. Another girl about whom, when they spoke of her, boys lowered their voices. I played basketball for about sixty seconds, and scored one goal. That's it for athletics. Learned what a blow-job was—very important. Suffered the terror of taking a shower in public. Suffering with or without some redemptive experience remains suffering, unless you mistakenly classify writing this as a redemptive act."

"You were in the band?"

"Yeah, I was playing the trumpet, although not very well. My music teacher was Sam Freeman, the leader of the American Legion Band. We used to play at various institutions, and on the steps of the Capitol early Easter morning. Got to high school. The music teacher, Charlie Danforth, nice enough guy, suggested I play the sousaphone because he needed sousaphones in the band, disingenuously suggesting that it would help my trumpet playing. I dutifully complied, and lugged that sinuous monster around for a couple of years. But nothing could help my trumpet playing—I just wasn't very good. Then he suggested I play the cello, because the orchestra needed cellos. I dutifully complied."

"Where were your parents in all these changes? They didn't step in?"

"They were inured to my habitual trying something and then quitting, so these changes fit into an established pattern. I'm sure they realized that such behavior signaled trouble, but they were not able to help, or willing to find help. As parents, they were handicapped. Being a parent requires empathy, and you can't be empathetic if you yourself are so needy, so uncomfortable in your own skin. Their lack of attention bordered on neglect—when my mother was sick, it *was* neglect. My father, apparently, had no idea how to help me look better—yet pictures from years before show he knew how to buy good stuff for himself at Roger's Peet. How is it that it was so hard to do for me? I think eighth grade was the year of the Brylcreem Pompadour. The shoving, noisy hallways were awful. I was into archery—yet another stupidity that I was happy to daydream about and to fail at—and did something in shop—I think I made a stencil that needed to be inked onto a T-shirt. What a great combination: archery, Brylcreem, and late puberty!"

"Where was your brother in all this?"

"He escaped to Philips Exeter in New Hampshire. A full scholarship, since we had little money. I worked seriously at the cello for several years, but it was not to be. I do remember auditioning for All State Orchestra, and taking whatever one-octave scale I was supposed to play through four octaves. I scored a 9.75 on a scale of 10. A victory, but it was too late—I was already beyond victories. Or maybe better, it was a victory in the wrong war."

Chapter XXXIII

Feather Time

own and feathers, colored and white—as we plucked the birds during slaughter, we kept the feathers separate by swapping in different bushel baskets. We threw out the larger feathers— they fetched too little to bother with. If we had time, part of the cleanup at the end of the day was putting the still-wet down into the burlap grain bags we always saved. Since the object was to dry the feathers as quickly as possible, we divided each basket among two or three bags. These were first hung in the attic, then taken down into the cellar, where we spread them out on the top of the hot air ducts leading from the furnace— we were always, it seemed, bringing into the house that which rightfully belonged outside. The down dried and fluffed, and the burlap feed sack was now the harsh husk of a giant pillow.

The relative inactivity of winter gave us time to further work on the feathers. Burlap was good for corn, but feed which tended to pulverize came in bags of coarse cotton, decorated in gaily printed patterns. These we washed and dried, and sometimes, opening one up completely, we produced two good dish towels by cutting it in half. It was into two of these, one inside the other for safety, that we poured the contents of ten or twelve of the original bags. The down that inevitably clung to the burlap had to be gathered up by hand . We worked on the cellar steps. My father was the stuffer and stood below the bag; Jeb and I stood higher and held open the mouth. He stuffed down firmly each infusion of feathers in order to make room for the next, such stuffing performed by taking a handful of feathers from the middle of the bag and forcing it down the side. Toward the end, there was no room to pour: he had to make the entire transfer by the handful. All this motion and stuffing caused gossamer filaments to float all over, like a burst milkweed pod in the fall. They clung to your hair and clothes, and the dust filled your nose. We used to vacuum ourselves off after one of these sessions. Months later, feathers still floated around the house.

The bag, near bursting from the three pounds in it and now firm as a junior punching bag, was securely tied, labeled, and taken to the Post Office. Other people took letters to the Post Office and were warmly greeted; we took bags of feathers, causing no end of respiratory problems for their employees. On seeing my father enter, the clerks' eyes began to water.

Why couldn't I be normal and have respiratory problems?

The bag was also too large, that is, the sum of the long and short girths was over the Post Office's limit. However, stuff as we might on the cellar stairs, there was always some give to the bag, and with a little good will and a modest tug on the postal clerk's tape, we just skinned under the limit.

White goose down brought $2.00 or more per pound; other down brought less. A check from the Chicago Feather Company arrived in a couple of weeks for $6.50.

Chapter XXXIV

Winter Chores

Banding, like feathers, was another ugly, weekend job, but in just one day it was done for the year. And unlike feathers, nothing from banding ever followed you to school, stuck to your sweater. The young birds and the breeder stock roamed freely together. We didn't want to slaughter the breeder stock; an old duck—well, you can eat it if you fricassee the daylights out of it. If a customer got one, he might not come back the following year. Geese were easier to classify: the older ganders were fearless—they hissed at you and refused to be intimidated.

We herded all the birds into the duck house, and caught them one by one, usually by two people running them into a corner. Catching them terrified the poor things. Those already wearing a band, its security checked, were immediately put out the door to the pen reserved for the breeding stock. At first we used brightly-colored, plastic rings, but found that the birds could worry them off, so we switched to metal bands with embossed numbers—much better suited to serious flock control. On those prime, young birds lucky enough to be selected as breeders we put one of these unshakable leg bands—snug but not too tight—and crimped back the tongue; these we let out into the pen, also. The rest were destined for somebody's table, or our freezer.

In winter, chores were a real pain. The duck house was unheated (actually it was air-conditioned year round, thanks to broken windows that were never fixed). Cold or no, animals need to drink, and waterfowl are particularly messy drinkers. Water, dribbling from the sides of their beaks, ran down the side of the pail, and, by accretion, formed an adobe-hard donut of ice, straw and manure which froze the pail to the floor. By the next chore-time, the rest of the water had frozen also. If you repeatedly yanked the pail off the floor, the bottom soon fell out. If you banged the pail on some hard surface, or worse, kicked the pathetic thing (showing annoyance was considered a sign of poor character) to loosen the ice, the sides became dented, and absent significant hot water, hot water heated on the stove and hand-carried from the kitchen, the ice would henceforth never slide out.

We shoveled snow—a lot of snow. The barn, where we parked the car in the winter, was about a hundred feet from the road. A big wooden scoop made the job much easier: you didn't have to lift the snow, one shovelful at a time, and so the actual depth of the snowfall made less difference. Run the wooden scoop under the snow, loosen a big cube, pull the load back, keeping it level, and dump it well clear of the driveway.

The end of the driveway was another matter. The heavy plows, by repeated passes, compacted the snow into high embankments, a section of which now thrust itself up before us like the Continental Divide. Sometimes it was impossible, because it was wet or frozen, to drive the scoop into it, despite its metal edge on the front: Jeb used a spade to break away sections of the hardened embankment, and I ran the scoop underneath the loosened snow. Where to put this snow also became a problem as the winter wore on. The road's embankments quickly rose too high even to consider shoveling snow over them, and late in the season the snow dumped at the sides of the driveway started to crowd in. Our solution: dump it in the road below the driveway, up against the embankment.

"You dumped your snow in the road? I thought the road was already plowed?"

"It was plowed, but plows make multiple passes: first to get the snow off the road, and then to push back the embankments."

"So you hoped for a secondary pass?"

"Yeah. That's why we put it *below* the driveway. Plows always operate with the traffic, so it was pushed harmlessly away, and not back in."

"But didn't they push *some* snow back in the driveway?"

"Yeah, we hated to hear them coming by again, although it made the snow we had dumped in the road in such an un-neighborly fashion vanish. But another, if smaller, windrow of plow-hardened snow was pushed into the end of the driveway, and our carefully-cut shoulders were ruined—at least the uphill one."

"What shoulders?"

"The shoulders of the end of the driveway. You couldn't just leave the driveway straight out to the road like an alley—the car needed some turning room. So we cut back these high shoulders. Spade work."

We also had to dig out the mailbox for the postman's car. If the plow did it, that is, the plow got close enough to your mailbox so the mailman could reach it, there was no mailbox for him to get to. What used to be your mailbox was in the ditch.

The city was very good about plowing our road. When the snow stopped, if you could get out of your driveway, you could almost always get to town. Except once, in February, 1952. Thirty inches of snow, sixty-mile-per-hour winds, fifteen-foot drifts. Regular plows were useless— only plows with V-shaped blades got through. The state stopped for a couple of days. School stopped for a week. The snow was over the top of some of our windows: the reduced daylight milky and opaque. We got the back door open. Shovel in hand, I decided to charge ahead. I stepped off the back steps and disappeared into a snow drift.

An endless stream of wild birds found their way into the duck house in the winter. They ate the grain, or maybe they ate the grain which dribbled to the floor—waterfowl are also messy shovelers. They annoyed us and we begrudged them every morsel, so we shot them. We shot them with air rifles, and we shot them with the .22 rifle. The .22 was better because, as they bunched cowering in one high corner of the duck house, one shot got three of them. The shot also went through the eves, ventilating the place still further, landing, I suppose, in one of the fields in the back. We never considered that someone might be *out* there. A better solution would have been to close the holes in the building and put wire mesh over the broken window, but we never did. The killing was done without anger or pleasure. They annoyed us. They ate the grain.

Chapter XXXV

Ernest Cunningham

The farm up the hill belonged to Ernest Cunningham. Property lines in Maine are always marked by a row of rocks and boulders, more often a sprawling pile than a wall; a fence is added if you have livestock. Like ours, his house ran back from the road in cobbled-on pieces—a kitchen, an ell, a shed—until it reached the corner of his barn, and so allowed him the luxury of getting to the cows without going outside in bad weather. Several other out-buildings of various sizes were scattered around, there for so long that their connection to the earth was no longer merely physical, but organic. His wife Pearl was a pleasant woman, overweight and palsied, and had trouble getting around. I don't remember any of the house except for the kitchen, which felt shrunk and rural, and smelled faintly of cow manure.

"Cow manure! How yucky!"

"We were never allowed to say 'yucky'; commenting on others' shortcomings was universally proscribed. Besides, it was inevitable, so then for sure we were not allowed to say anything."

"How do you mean? Couldn't he change his clothes out in the barn, or something?"

"Wouldn't have done any good. You remember Ray Andrews?"

"Not really."

"Ray Andrews had to help muck out the cows before school and also smelled faintly of cow manure. I'm sure he washed his hands and face and changed his clothes before school, but the smell gets in your hair and skin, like working in a pickle factory. You cannot wash it off."

"How awful. Then he had to ride on the bus and sit next to kids from town. Ended up a social outcast probably."

"He seemed to bear it all right, but you never know. By the time he was a freshman, Roger, his younger brother, got the mucking-out job, and he moved up to milking. That must have provided some relief. Next year they went to milking machines—better yet."

Ernest's barn was an imposing affair, as high as a three-story house; along one wall was the tie-up for the cows. Across from the tie-up was a separate building for the horses, and slightly further up the hill, the milk room, with running water to wash out the cans and pails, a milk cooler, and a hand-cranked milk separator into whose spinning, stainless-steel bowl Ernest poured whole milk: from one spout came the skim, and from the other the cream.

"How'd that thing work?"
"I don't know: seems like magic, but—you've never seen unhomogenized milk?—the cream floats to the top of the bottle. So it must be lighter—like oil, and somehow the machine, using centrifugal force, took advantage of the variation. It was very cool."
"How much cream was there?"
"Down into the shoulder of a glass milk bottle—about a third of the way down. We had to shake it up."
"What'd he do with the skim milk?"
"Slopped the pigs with it, I think."

Ernest put up several bottles of milk for us from each night's milking. One of my chores in the evening was to go up to the milk house and get it. I sometimes forgot, and apparently so did everyone one else. They were all so clever—why didn't they remember? The milk froze. The bottle broke. Sometimes I remembered after I had my pajamas on. "Oh my God, the milk!" No one still dressed for winter ever volunteered to go. I threw on a jacket, found my mittens, bare feet in rubber pacs, and with nothing on the my legs except thin pajama bottoms, hustled up the hill, grabbed the bottle, and flew home.

Several times Ernest hitched up a horse to the sleigh and trotted smartly down the snow-covered road. It was the real thing, bells and all, with a stiff, smelly bear skin to cover your legs. He was born in 1886 and had lived in the same house since 1912. He had worked in the woods with Civil War veterans cutting elm trees three feet thick at the stump with nothing but an axe and a crosscut saw, bucking the logs out with a team of horses, rolling them with long peaveys with big hooks and heavy handles—

"What's a peavey?"

"Has a long handle of wood inserted into a steel socket, the socket coming to a point. Bolted to the steel is a very large hook with a sharp point. This hook swings freely back and forth, so the tool is effective over a wide range of tree diameters. You trap the tree between the hook on the back side of a log and the point on the front, and the leverage thus obtained makes it extremely powerful. Named after the guy who invented it. Factory is up near Bangor—Eddington, I think."

He had lived a long time and had many stories. Hard work and little money had been a way of life. At age seventy he could see two porcupines kissing at 3,000 feet, and fill a glass milk bottle from a ten-quart pail without spilling a drop.

"Quite a life. Did you ever write a story about him?"

"No, I never got a family history from him, a missed opportunity that I will always regret."

"Maybe your father got . . ."

"No, he missed the story, too. I was young, so maybe I can be forgiven, but he knew a story when he saw one, and there was one living right next door. He screwed up, and Ernest's world is gone forever."

"Except for Christmas and the sleigh!"

"Just mythology now, is all it is. Almost all the people who sing songs about sleighs at Christmas have never seen one. But I still feel bad about him. I abandoned him, alas. People disappear—"

"In what way?"

"I guess it was the summer between my junior and senior year in high school, or maybe it was the summer before—I really don't remember. No, it couldn't have been: I went to New England Music Camp that summer. Anyway, when haying came, I just didn't show up. I busied myself practicing, and—this is such painful nonsense—hid behind the need to protect my hands (a belief I got from my mother), so I couldn't do all that heavy work. But then it seems like the same summer I was at a different haying operation, attempting to throw heavy bales up onto a truck. Then I moved away, college, the Army—I never came back for a visit."

"Too bad."

"And there's another reason that weighs heavily on me. He was one of the few people who befriended my parents when they had no friends. God! I think he would have laid down his life for us. And he's no longer here to thank. Like the people who helped us when my mother was sick, which I only learned about recently: a turkey from the American Legion, the local undertaker lent her a wheelchair gratis, food from the Salvation Army, clothes and such from some welfare organization in town—no one now to thank."

His wife was very sick at the end of her life; he took care of her. Dr. Mollison, who had helped my mother, came over every day, and, without pay, changed the dressing on her ulcers. Ernest defended our family when the FBI came around and asked their nosey questions. Once, when two agents came out to the haying operation, he pointed to us and said "Those boys, help me every summer, they work hard. Wonderful boys. Wish I had 'em." When I got sick, he cried. I worked with him all the years of growing up. I was sure I knew everything about him I needed to know. I now know little more than where he is buried.

Epilogue

I have dreams in which I am attempting to purchase the land of the different places where we lived. They are of immense value. All over, the woods are reclaiming the fields because no one mows them. Their old forms, so tactile in memory, merge and fit together like some enormous puzzle. But pieces of other puzzles have gotten mixed in: the old and the new often fit together poorly, if at all. The sorting out is never finished.

CPSIA information can be obtained
at www.ICGtesting.com
Printed in the USA
BVOW06s1132220118
505965BV00006B/670/P